T0302101

Forging Ahead, Falling Behind and Fighting Back

To what extent has the British economy declined compared to its competitors and what are the underlying reasons for this decline? Nicholas Crafts, one of the world's foremost economic historians, tackles these questions in a major new account of Britain's long-run economic performance. He argues that history matters in interpreting current economic performance, because the present is always conditioned by what went before. Bringing together ideas from economic growth theory and varieties of capitalism to endogenous growth and cliometrics, he reveals the microeconomic foundations of Britain's economic performance in terms of the impact of institutional arrangements and policy choices on productivity performance. The book traces Britain's path from the First Industrial Revolution and global economic primacy through its subsequent long-term decline, the strengths and weaknesses of the Thatcherite response and the improvement in relative economic performance that was sustained to the eve of the financial crisis.

NICHOLAS CRAFTS is Professor of Economic History at the University of Warwick. His many publications include *The Great Depression of the 1930s: Lessons for Today* (2013), co-edited with Peter Fearon, *Work and Pay in Twentieth Century Britain* (2007), co-edited with Ian Gazeley and Andrew Newell, and *British Economic Growth During the Industrial Revolution* (1985).

Forging Ahead, Falling Behind and Fighting Back

British Economic Growth from the Industrial Revolution to the Financial Crisis

NICHOLAS CRAFTS

University of Warwick

CAMBRIDGE
UNIVERSITY PRESS

CAMBRIDGE
UNIVERSITY PRESS

University Printing House, Cambridge CB2 8BS, United Kingdom

One Liberty Plaza, 20th Floor, New York, NY 10006, USA

477 Williamstown Road, Port Melbourne, VIC 3207, Australia

314-321, 3rd Floor, Plot 3, Splendor Forum, Jasola District Centre, New Delhi - 110025, Ind

79 Anson Road, #06-04/06, Singapore 079906

Cambridge University Press is part of the University of Cambridge.

It furthers the University's mission by disseminating knowledge in the pursuit of education, learning and research at the highest international levels of excellence.

www.cambridge.org
Information on this title: www.cambridge.org/9781108424400
DOI: 10.1017/9781108334907

© Nicholas Crafts 2018

First published 2018

A catalogue record for this publication is available from the British Library

ISBN 978-1-108-42440-0 Hardback
ISBN 978-1-108-43816-2 Paperback

Contents

Figures and Tables

Acknowledgements

This book has been developed from the Ellen McArthur Lectures which I gave at the University of Cambridge in 2009. I was honoured by the invitation to give the lectures. The opportunity encouraged me further to explore themes in my research which had not previously been thought through, especially with regard to the implication of Britain's early start as an industrial nation.

When I presented the lectures I received excellent support from Martin Daunton and Leigh Shaw-Taylor. Martin Daunton and Tim Leunig read a draft of the book and made valuable suggestions. Michael Watson at Cambridge University Press has been supportive throughout and has been astonishingly patient with my slow progress in delivering the manuscript. I am grateful to all of them.

I Introduction

This book examines the British economy's growth performance over the last 250 years. The focal point is to offer an interpretation – informed by ideas from growth economics, and firmly grounded in empirical evidence – of the relative economic decline that characterized the period from the mid-nineteenth century, when Britain had the highest per capita income of any major economy, to the early 1980s, when this had fallen below the West-European average. This will entail an analysis of the experience of economic growth from the Industrial Revolution to the eve of the financial crisis which erupted in 2007.

The concept of 'relative economic decline' relates to international comparisons of the level of real Gross Domestic Product (GDP) per person. As applied to Britain, it means that over many decades economic growth was slower than in a peer group of other countries, with the result that they first caught up, and then overtook, British income levels. As is reported in Table 1.1, this describes the economic history of the post-Industrial Revolution period through the 1970s. Relative economic decline was most apparent vis-à-vis the United States, from the American Civil War to 1950 and, compared with European countries, during the 1950s to the 1970s.

Relative economic decline did not mean that British economic growth slowed down. On the contrary, as is shown in Table 1.2, the long-run tendency was for the rate of growth of real GDP per person to increase over time. The acceleration in economic growth which Britain experienced as result of the Industrial Revolution represents the transition to 'modern economic growth' (Kuznets, 1966) where technological progress took centre stage. From the Industrial Revolution to the First World War, growth averaged a little under

1

Table 1.1 *Real GDP/person (UK = 100 in each year)*

	USA	Germany	France
1820	65.6	51.9	54.7
1870	76.6	57.6	58.8
1913	107.7	74.1	70.8
1929	125.3	73.6	85.6
1937	103.4	75.3	72.2
1950	137.8	61.7	74.7
1979	142.7	115.9	111.1
2007	132.9	107.0	98.6

Notes: Estimates refer to West Germany in 1950 and 1979.
Purchasing power parity estimates in $1990GK for 1870–1979
and in $2015EKS for 2007.
Sources: Maddison (2010) and The Conference Board (2016).

Table 1.2 *Growth rates of real GDP, population and real GDP/person (% per year)*

	GDP	Population	Real GDP /person
1500–1650	0.59	0.60	–0.01
1650–1780	0.71	0.24	0.47
1780–1820	1.43	1.22	0.21
1820–1870	2.12	1.24	0.88
1870–1913	1.90	0.89	1.01
1929–1937	1.99	0.44	1.55
1950–1979	2.63	0.40	2.23
1979–2007	2.54	0.32	2.22

Note: Estimates based on England up to 1700, Britain 1700–1870,
United Kingdom 1870–2007.
Sources: Broadberry et al. (2015) and The Maddison Project database.

1 per cent per year, roughly double the rate from 1650 to 1780 – itself
well above the 0.2 per cent average over the previous 400 years – but
less than half that achieved since the Second World War. The problem

was rather that growth in other countries increased by more than in Britain as faster technological advance became possible.

Evidently, growth comparisons, whether inter-temporal or international, need to be handled with care. It is important to take into account what is feasible, and to recognize that relative economic decline does not always connote 'failure'. It seems clear that the accumulation of knowledge and human capital characteristic of the last 100 years has been conducive to faster technological progress in the advanced economies, as is reflected in their capacity to exploit major new technologies increasingly quickly (Crafts, 2012). Growth of real GDP per person of around 2 per cent per year was not feasible in 1800 but quite normal 200 years later. Similarly, growth possibilities may vary across countries at a point in time because of different scope for catch-up or the 'inappropriateness' of technological change.

The former is widely recognized and with the availability of purchasing power parity adjusted series for relative income levels can now be taken properly into account. Countries grow faster when they embark on catch-up from an initially low income and productivity level. No Western European country could expect to grow at a double-digit pace as China has in the recent past. Equally, Britain as the first industrial nation, could expect to be caught up as modern economic growth spread – reflected in relative economic decline compared with European countries in the nineteenth century. On the other hand, being overtaken by its European peer group, as happened to Britain in the 1960s and 1970s, surely is a diagnostic of a growth failure since there is no reason to think that other countries had access to superior technology or a more favourable geography.

Adoption of a new technology is not always appropriate – it may be profitable in some countries but not others because cost or demand conditions differ. It follows that different technological choices may be rational and the technological playing field may not be level. The appropriateness of technology may be affected by relative factor prices perhaps differing on account of geography or the level of development. It is widely remarked that this is an important issue in the viability of technologies developed by advanced economies for adoption in poor developing countries (Allen, 2012). But, in past times, appropriateness was relevant to the diffusion of technology between leading economies both with regard to other countries' ability to emulate Britain at the time of the Industrial Revolution, and in terms of American technology's suitability for adoption in Europe at the time of the 'second Industrial Revolution' a hundred years later.

Growth economics now offers valuable analytical tools with which to develop an explanation for relative economic decline which was not really the case when the traditional neoclassical economic growth model ruled the roost. This viewed the sources of economic growth as growth in the capital stock and the labour force, and improvements in technology which raised the productivity of these inputs. This model has two key assumptions, namely, that capital accumulation is subject to diminishing returns and that technological progress is exogenous and universally available. These assumptions are fundamental to two well-known predictions of the model about the long run, namely, that increasing the rate of investment has no effect on the steady-state rate of economic growth and that all countries converge to the same income level as initially backward countries automatically enjoy rapid catch-up growth.[1]

Although some insights from this model have found favour (and an empirical technique derived from it, growth accounting, has been widely used in economic history) it is fair to say that the pure neoclassical model has been regarded by most economic historians, as unhelpful much of the time. In particular, the notions of universal technology and long-run income convergence have seemed far-fetched to scholars accustomed to thinking in terms of, say, the new institutional economic history with its emphasis on the importance of institutions and political economy considerations to growth outcomes. Moreover, this model cannot really cope with the leading economy being overtaken and, after all, this is at the heart of Britain's relative economic decline.

---

[1]   The model can easily be adapted to allow for improvements in labour quality from better education without changing these basic predictions.

The so-called 'new' growth economics offers models with more attractive features. These include acceptance that institutions and policy can affect the growth rate, and can promote divergence in growth outcomes and, associated with this, the recognition that catching-up is not automatic. The most useful of these new models embody the idea of endogenous innovation; they consider that technological advance, whether through invention or diffusion, is influenced by economic incentives, in particular, expected profitability and they drop the assumption that technology is universal. Technologies are developed to address market demands in particular locations and may not be appropriate elsewhere (Acemoglu, 1998). Carefully deployed, these ideas can inform an appraisal of controversies surrounding British growth performance.

Broadly speaking, new growth economics suggests that there are two important aspects of the incentive structures that influence the decisions to invest and to innovate which matter for growth outcomes, namely, their impact on expected returns and on agency problems (Aghion and Howitt, 1998). Thus, institutions and policies that reduce the supply price of capital or research inputs, or reduce fears of expropriation, can increase innovative effort, speed up technology transfer and enhance the chances of rapid catch-up growth. Innovative effort is also positively affected by greater market size, which makes it easier to cover the fixed costs of innovating. Since effective and timely adoption of new technologies tends to be costly to the management of firms in terms of the effort required, it is also important that managers are incentivized to work hard on behalf of the owners – when this is not the case we speak of performance being jeopardized by principal–agent problems. Unless there are large external shareholders who can internalize the benefits of effective control of management, strong (though less than perfect) competition tends to be important in underpinning TFP growth (Nickell, 1996).

These ideas also resonate with economic historians' discussions of the international diffusion of technology. In particular, there is an obvious connection with the idea of 'social capability' used by Abramovitz and David (1996). But it should also be noted that these authors also stress the importance of 'technological congruence' in catching up or falling behind. Here the point is that the cost-effectiveness of a technology may vary across countries where demand or cost conditions are different. An interesting aspect of this, as pointed out by Abramovitz (1986) is that social capability is not an absolute but may vary according to the technology in question – for example, institutions and policies which were excellent for the diffusion of Fordist production techniques in manufacturing in the 1950s, may not be ideal to facilitate rapid uptake of ICT in services in the 1990s.

The key ideas are captured in Figure 1.1, which is adapted from Carlin and Soskice (2006). In this figure x is the rate of (labour-augmenting) technological progress and ǩ is the capital to effective labour ratio. The upward-sloping (Schumpeter) line reflects the endogeneity of technological progress based on the assumption a larger market increases innovative effort because it is potentially more profitable, since success will be rewarded by greater sales. With more

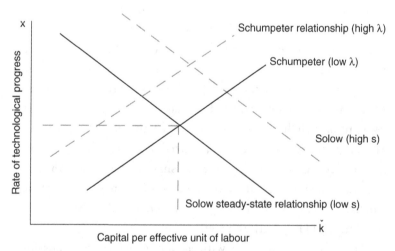

FIGURE 1.1: Endogenous growth

capital per unit of effective labour there will be higher income per person so the Schumpeter line is upward-sloping. The downward-sloping (Solow) line represents points which are consistent with the steady-state relationship between technological progress and capital per effective unit of labour. The steady-state is characterized by balanced growth in which the capital stock grows at the same rate as the sum of labour force growth and the rate of technological progress. When this is the case the capital to output ratio is constant and so is the ratio of capital to an effective unit of labour. For a given savings rate, the growth of the capital stock is faster the lower the capital to output ratio. With a 'well-behaved' production function, lower capital per effective unit of labour means a lower capital to output ratio. Thus, the Solow line will be downward sloping. The equilibrium rate of technological progress is established by the intersection of these two lines.

Figure 1.1 implies that the rate of innovation increases when either the Solow and/or the Schumpeter line shifts upward. An upward shift of the Solow line will be the result of an increased rate of savings (and investment) which will lead to faster technological progress and, thus, a faster rate of economic growth. In turn, investment will respond to changes in the economic environment which affect its expected profitability. An upward shift of the Schumpeter line associated with a 'higher λ', i.e., an increase in innovative effort for any given market size, will reflect such changes as greater technological opportunity, lower R & D costs, more appropriable returns from R & D and intensified competitive pressure on managers. Improvements in social capability and/or technological congruence can also be thought of as equivalent to a higher λ. The key implication of Figure 1.1 is that the growth rate will be affected by institutions and policies both through their impact on technological progress and on investment.

It is important to remember that as the twentieth century progressed, the United Kingdom increasingly obtained its new technology from abroad. The key to growth performance became prompt and effective diffusion of foreign technology rather than domestic invention. Technological opportunity from advances in other leading countries, and the social capability to exploit them, is what mattered most. In an open economy, greater success in technology transfer will raise λ.

Key points in the chapters that follow can be situated within the framework of Figure 1.1. Thus, the discussion of the Industrial Revolution in Chapter 2 highlights that there was a much lower rate of technological progress than was traditionally believed, and provides reasons why λ and s were still quite low in an economy where institutions and economic policies left a good deal to be desired. Conversely, in Chapter 3 where American overtaking is discussed, a number of reasons why the United States had become a relatively high-λ economy are discussed. These include market size, investments in human capital and technological opportunities not available to European countries. In Chapter 4, it is noted that these advantages persisted as the United States continued to heavily outperform Britain during the interwar period.

Figure 1.1 is particularly helpful in Chapter 5's analysis of the Golden Age of catch-up growth after the Second World War when both the Schumpeter and Solow lines were subject to favourable shifts in many countries. Technological progress in Europe was boosted by increased opportunities for technology transfer, while in coordinated market economies saving and investment were increased by cooperative agreements between firms and workers. On the other hand, Britain found that λ was reduced by institutional legacies and policy errors. In the later twentieth century, as discussed in Chapter 6, the scope for catch-up growth had declined and there were downward shifts in both the Schumpeter and Solow lines. Britain's relative performance improved somewhat, however, as institutional and policy reforms had a positive impact on λ.

Economic historians might want to add something quite distinctive to ideas from conventional growth economics so as to emphasize that 'history matters' in the sense that the past constrains and shapes the present, and that 'path dependence' is a relevant idea (David, 1994).[2] North (2005) stressed path dependence in the context of institutional change and failures of reform in which inefficient institutions persist, and 'status-quo bias' can also inhibit policy reform (Fernandez and Rodrik, 1991). This is potentially an important issue as countries pass from the early to later stages of development, or as the world moves from one technological epoch to another and reform is desirable. Aghion and Howitt (2006) emphasized that the policies appropriate for a 'far-from-frontier' and a 'close-to-frontier' economy may differ greatly, echoing the insights of Gerschenkron (1962). In the British context, these ideas can be explored in the context of making sense of the long-standing claim in the literature that the 'early start' impaired subsequent growth performance.

The legacy of the past can cast its shadow over economic performance in a number of other ways. In an open economy, the structure of production depends on relative productivity compared with trading partners. This may be influenced by the development of large agglomerations which have surprising staying power – cotton textiles in Lancashire at the turn of the twentieth century come immediately to mind. The strength of successful sectors 'crowds out' other activities and inhibits the development of new, ultimately more dynamic, sectors as with so-called 'Dutch disease'. Policy choices may not only be constrained by the vested interests inherited from, or the 'inescapable experience' of the past, but there are also interaction effects between institutional legacies and policy changes – for example the 'British system of industrial relations' had important implications for the impact on productivity of the weakening of competition, which resulted from the difficulties of the 1930s.

---

[2] Path dependence is a property of non-ergodic stochastic processes whose asymptotic distributions evolve as a history of the process itself. So the vision of history is that in a multiple-equilibrium world it is possible to get locked into a locally stable equilibrium (which may be inferior) by historical accident.

With these ideas in mind, the rest of the book reviews Britain's growth performance over the long run, starting with the experience of the Industrial Revolution. The aim is not so much to provide a textbook account, but to develop an analytic perspective. This will entail providing description, explanation and evaluation of the growth record in successive periods. The analysis will be firmly grounded in economics, but will recognize the importance of historical context and the ways in which economic performance is conditioned by what went before. I shall feel free to engage with major debates in the historiography and bold enough to draw some 'lessons from history'.

2 The First Industrial Revolution

The term 'Industrial Revolution' is commonly used to characterize the unprecedented experience of the British economy during the later decades of the eighteenth and early decades of the nineteenth century. Taken literally, it is a misleading phrase, but carefully deployed, it is a useful metaphor. These years saw a remarkable economic achievement by comparison with earlier times but it must be recognized that by later standards this was in many ways a modest beginning. Moreover, the basis on which initial success was accomplished would not be sufficient to sustain leadership over the long run.

The idea of an 'industrial revolution' conjures up images of spectacular technological breakthroughs, the triumph of the factory system, rapid economic growth and the industrialization of an economy based largely on agriculture hitherto. Indeed, these were the directions of travel for the British economy but, when they are quantified, the numbers, although impressive once put into context, do not live up to the hyperbole. For several decades, while the economy withstood formidable demographic pressure much better than could have been imagined in the seventeenth century, the growth of real income per person was painfully slow. Not much more than a third of the labour force worked in agriculture in the mid-eighteenth century. In 1851, more people were employed in domestic service and distribution than in textiles, metals and machine-making combined. Until about 1830 water power was more important than steam power in British industry.

Nevertheless, the economy of the mid-nineteenth century was established on a different trajectory from that of a hundred years earlier. In particular, sustained labour productivity growth based on steady technological progress and higher levels of investment had become the basis of significant growth in real income per person notwithstanding rapid population growth. This was 'modern economic growth' rather than an economy where real income increases were based on Smithian growth and working more days per year. That said, growth potential was still quite limited by twentieth-century standards in an economy where education and scientific capabilities were still quite primitive, the scope to import technological advances from the rest of the world was modest and institutions and economic policies had obvious limitations.

This picture has become conventional as quantification of British economic performance has progressed over the past fifty years or so. What remains much less clear is to what extent and when, if at all, the development of the British economy during this period made subsequent modernization more difficult and impaired growth later on. As will become apparent, the early start did entail the emergence of some idiosyncratic features which became an unusual legacy for later generations.

2.1   AN OVERVIEW OF GROWTH AND STRUCTURAL CHANGE

The dimensions of economic growth and structural change during the Industrial Revolution have emerged from a long process of research starting with Deane and Cole (1962) and culminating in Broadberry et al. (2013) and Broadberry et al. (2015). These recent publications have improved significantly the estimates in Crafts (1985). It is also now possible to locate this experience in a well-articulated intertemporal and international context.

Table 2.1 shows that the income levels reached in Britain in the mid-nineteenth century were much higher than anything achieved in Britain or elsewhere in earlier centuries, and that by then Britain had overtaken the earlier European leaders, Italy and the Netherlands. The long period of slow growth before the Industrial Revolution and the 'Great Divergence' between the European leaders and China can be clearly seen. The British economy managed to

Table 2.1 *Real GDP/person, 1086–1850 ($1990GK)*

	England/ Great Britain	Holland/ Netherlands	Italy	Spain	China
1086	754				1244
1348	777	876	1376	1030	
1400	1090	1245	1601	885	948
1500	1114	1483	1403	889	909
1600	1123	2372	1244	944	852
1650	1100	2171	1271	820	
1700	1630/1563	2403	1350	880	843
1750	1710	2440	1403	910	737
1800	2080	2617/1752	1244	962	639
1850	2997	2397	1350	1144	600

Source: Broadberry (2013).

sustain the jump in income levels consequent on the Black Death and from 1650 to 1780, real GDP per person grew at about 0.5 per cent per year (Table 2.1), a rate which had more than doubled by the mid-nineteenth century. The 1650–1780 rate of growth of real GDP had tripled from 0.7 to 2.1 per cent per year by 1820–1870, enough to outstrip the rise in population growth from 0.2 to 1.2 per cent per year. This rate of population growth would have implied serious pressure on living standards in earlier centuries. From that vantage point, the remarkable aspect of the Industrial Revolution period was that real income per person did not fall significantly; this 'dog that didn't bark' indicates that the economy had escaped from the Malthusian Trap.

Of course, the growth of industrial production was appreciably faster than that of GDP because it outpaced growth in agriculture and services. Between 1780 and 1860, industrial output grew at 2.6 per cent per year compared with 0.6 per cent for agriculture, 2.0 per cent for services and 1.9 per cent for real GDP (Broadberry et al., 2015). The most rapidly expanding industries had much faster growth but, especially at first, were quite small relative to the economy as a whole; cotton textiles output grew by 6.4 per cent per year

Table 2.2 *Shares of world industrial production (%)*

	1750	1830	1860	1880	1913
Britain	1.9	9.5	19.9	22.9	13.6
Rest Western Europe	15.2	18.1	25.4	30.0	33.9
United States	0.1	2.5	7.2	14.7	32.0
China	32.8	29.8	19.5	12.5	3.6
India	24.5	17.6	8.6	2.7	1.4

Source: Bairoch (1982).

Table 2.3 *Sectoral shares in employment (%)*

	Agriculture	Industry	Services
1522	58.1	22.7	19.2
1700	38.9	34.0	27.2
1759	36.8	33.9	29.3
1801	31.7	36.4	31.9
1851	23.5	45.6	30.9

Note: England in 1522, Britain thereafter.
Source: Broadberry et al. (2013).

between 1780 and 1860 (Deane and Cole, 1962). Table 2.2 reports an estimate that Britain accounted for just less than 20 per cent of world industrial output by 1860 – similar to China whose population was about thirteen times Britain's – at a time when Britain produced roughly 40 per cent of world manufactured exports. Statistics such as these make the common description of Britain as the 'workshop of the world' understandable, if somewhat over the top.

By the mid-nineteenth century, Britain was highly industrialized with 45 per cent of employment in industry (Table 2.3). The structure of employment had been transformed compared with Elizabethan times. However, recent research has made clear that a good deal of this switch towards industry had already occurred prior to the Industrial Revolution (Shaw-Taylor, 2009) and that employment in mid-eighteenth-century Britain was less agricultural and more industrial than was supposed in Crafts (1985), especially when female employment is properly taken into account. It is still entirely valid to see Britain as an outlier in the mid-nineteenth century by virtue of its very low share of agricultural employment based on the disappearance of peasant agriculture and the trade of an open economy which imported a significant fraction of its food and had a strong position in manufactured exports (Crafts and Harley, 2004), but, although structural change speeded up during the Industrial Revolution period, it was less dramatic than used to be thought.

A major implication of the revised employment estimates is a different (and more plausible) pattern of sectoral contributions to labour productivity growth from that presented in Crafts (1985). Table 2.4 shows that industrial labour productivity growth was considerably faster between 1759 and 1851, although well below the rate estimated by Deane and Cole (1962), and was also well above that of agriculture. The weakness of overall labour productivity growth during the classic Industrial Revolution period is quite striking and, at one level, explains why living standards of many workers stagnated during these years.

Table 2.4 *Labour productivity growth, 1700–1851 (% per year)*

	Agriculture	Industry	GDP
1700–1759	0.59	0.16	0.31
1759–1801	0.24	0.63	0.34
1801–1851	0.01	0.96	0.64
1801–1831	–0.33	0.68	0.24

Notes: Productivity on a per worker basis.
Sources: Derived from Broadberry et al. (2013) and Broadberry et al. (2015) with labour force shares in 1831 interpolated.

2.2 ACCOUNTING FOR GROWTH DURING THE INDUSTRIAL REVOLUTION

Changes in the sources of growth of labour productivity can be examined more systematically using the concept of growth accounting which has been widely employed by economic historians to benchmark performance (Crafts, 2009). The basic approach assumes that GDP is accounted for by the employment of factor inputs and their productivity Total Factor Productivity (TFP) as follows:

$$Y = AK^{\alpha}L^{\beta}N^{\gamma}$$

where Y is output, K is capital, L is labour, N is land and A is TFP while α, β and γ are the elasticities of output with respect to capital, labour and land, respectively. The level of TFP reflects the state of technology and it is usually measured as a residual after the other items in the expression have been measured. This can be converted into an equation to account for the proximate sources of output growth

$$\Delta Y/Y = \alpha\Delta K/K + \beta\Delta L/L + \gamma\Delta N/N + \Delta A/A$$

and a growth accounting equation for labour productivity growth

$$\Delta\ln(Y/L) = \alpha\Delta\ln(K/L) + \gamma\Delta\ln(N/L) + \Delta\ln A$$

The latter gives a decomposition of the percentage rate of growth of labour productivity into a contribution from the percentage rate of growth of capital per labour input (capital deepening), of land per labour input (land deepening) and a term based on the percentage growth rate of TFP. In implementing this approach in Table 2.5, it is assumed that factor shares are a reasonable approximation for the output elasticities.

Table 2.5 reports that the rate of TFP growth nearly doubled from 0.4 per cent per year in 1760–1800 to 0.7 per cent per year in 1830–1860. This certainly can be interpreted as reflecting acceleration in the rate of technological progress but TFP growth captures more

Table 2.5 *Growth accounting estimates (% per year)*

(a) *Output growth*

	Capital inputs contribution	Labour inputs contribution	Land inputs contribution	TFP growth	Real GDP growth
1760–1800	0.35*1.0 = 0.35	0.50*0.8 = 0.40	0.15*0.5 = 0.08	0.4	1.2
1800–1830	0.35*1.7 = 0.60	0.50*1.4 = 0.70	0.15*0.1 = 0.02	0.4	1.7
1830–1860	0.35*2.5 = 0.88	0.50*1.4 = 0.70	0.15*0.1 = 0.02	0.7	2.3

(b) *Labour productivity growth*

	K/L growth	N/L growth	TFP growth	Y/L growth
1760–1800	0.35*0.2 = 0.07	0.15*–0.3 = –0.04	0.4	0.4
1800–1830	0.35*0.3 = 0.10	0.15*–1.3 = –0.20	0.4	0.3
1830–1860	0.35*1.1 = 0.38	0.15*–1.3 = –0.20	0.7	0.9

Note: All estimates are derived on standard neoclassical assumptions with the weights as follows: capital = 0.35, land = 0.15, labour = 0.5.
Sources: Crafts (1985), (2005) revised with land growth from Allen (2009b) and real GDP growth based on Broadberry et al. (2015).

than this. No explicit allowance has been made for human capital in the growth accounting equation. Prior to 1830, it is generally agreed that any contribution from extra schooling or improved literacy was negligible, but in the period 1830–60 education may have accounted for around 0.3 percentage points per year of the measured TFP growth in Table 2.5 (Mitch, 1999). From 1760 to 1800, there is good reason to think that average hours worked per worker per year were increasing which is not taken into account in Table 2.5; the increase was probably enough to imply a correction to labour inputs growth sufficient to push TFP growth from technological progress down quite close to zero (Voth, 2001). More generally, it seems very likely that much of the increase in real GDP per person from the mid-fifteenth to the late eighteenth centuries came from people working longer rather than from technological advance (Broadberry et al., 2015, pp. 260–265). Overall then, a best guess might be that the contribution of technological progress, as reflected in TFP growth, went from about zero to a sustained rate of about 0.4 per cent per year by the time the classic Industrial Revolution period was completed.

At first sight, this may seem to undermine McCloskey's claim that 'ingenuity rather than abstention governed the industrial revolution' (1981, p. 108) which was made at a time when Deane and Cole's estimates of economic growth during the Industrial Revolution were the conventional wisdom and, based on these numbers, Feinstein (1981) estimated TFP growth of 1.3 per cent per year during 1801–1830. Replacing Deane and Cole's growth estimates with my 1985 figures and even more so with the revisions by Broadberry et al. (2015) leads to much lower TFP growth estimates, as we have seen, and an estimate that TFP growth contributes only about 30 per cent of output growth even in 1830–1860. However, if, as is more appropriate, the focus is on the sources of labour productivity growth, then it is immediately apparent that McCloskey was right and that TFP growth rather than physical-capital deepening accounted for the lion's share of labour productivity growth (Table 2.5).

Neoclassical growth accounting of this kind is a standard technique and valuable for benchmarking purposes, if nothing else. However, it does potentially underestimate the contribution of new technology to economic growth if technological progress is embodied in new types of capital goods, as was set out in detail by Barro (1999). This was surely the case during the Industrial Revolution; as Feinstein put it, 'many forms of technological advance ... can only take place when "embodied" in new capital goods. The spinning jennies, steam engines and blast furnaces were the "embodiment" of the industrial revolution' (1981, p. 142).

Table 2.6 *Contributions to labour productivity growth, 1780–1860 (% per year)*

Capital deepening	0.20
Modernized sectors	0.11
Other sectors	0.09
TFP growth	0.51
Modernized sectors	0.34
Other sectors	0.17
Labour productivity growth	0.71
Memorandum items	
Labour force growth	1.22
Capital income share (%)	35
Modernized sectors	5.2

Note: Derived using standard neoclassical growth accounting formula modified to allow for two types of capital. Modernized sectors are textiles, iron and transport.
Source: Crafts (2004a) updated to incorporate new output growth estimates from Broadberry et al. (2015) and revised to a three-factor growth accounting framework.

To allow for embodiment effects and to capture the idea of 'revolutionized' activities, it is possible to modify a growth accounting equation to distinguish between different types of capital and different sectors, along the following lines

$$\Delta\ln(Y/L) = \alpha_O\Delta\ln(K_O/L) + \alpha_N\Delta\ln(K_N/L) + \gamma\Delta\ln A_O + \Phi\Delta\ln A_N$$

where the subscripts O and N denote capital in the old and new sectors, respectively, γ and Φ are the gross output shares of these sectors, and α_O and α_N are the factor shares of the capital used in these sectors.[1] Disaggregation can be taken as far as the data permit.

Table 2.6 shows the results of an exercise of this kind. The 'modernized sectors' (cottons, woollens, iron, canals, ships and railways) are found to have contributed 0.45 out of 0.71 per cent per year

---

[1]   The terms γ and Φ are the so-called Domar weights which sum to greater than 1. For an algebraic justification of this procedure, see Hulten (1978).

growth in labour productivity over the period 1780–1860 with the majority of this, 0.34 compared with 0.11 per cent, coming from TFP growth as opposed to capital deepening. If the contribution of technological change to the growth of labour productivity is taken to be capital deepening in the modernized sectors plus total TFP growth, then this equates to 0.62 out of 0.71 per cent per year. It remains perfectly reasonable, therefore, to regard technological innovation as responsible for the acceleration in labour productivity growth that marked the importance of the Industrial Revolution as an historical discontinuity as Kuznets would have supposed even though the change was less dramatic than used to be thought.

It may seem surprising that the Industrial Revolution delivered such a modest rate of technological progress given the inventions for which it is famous including most obviously those related to the arrival of steam as a general purpose technology. It should be noted, however, that the well-known stagnation of real wage rates during this period is strong corroborative evidence that TFP growth, which is equal to the weighted average of growth in factor rewards (Barro, 1999), was modest.

Two points can be made straightaway. First, the impact of technological progress was very uneven as is implied by the estimates in Table 2.6. Most of the service sector other than transport was largely unaffected. Textiles, metals and machine-making accounted for less than a third of industrial employment – or 13.4 per cent of total employment – even in 1851 (Shaw-Taylor, 2009) and much industrial employment was still in 'traditional' sectors. Second, the process of technological advance was characterized by many incremental improvements and learning to realize the potential of the original inventions. This took time in an era where scientific and technological capabilities were still very weak by later standards.

Steam power offers an excellent example. The estimates in Table 2.7 show that its impact on productivity growth before 1830 was trivial – as was made clear by the detailed quantitative research of von Tunzelmann (1978) and Kanefsky (1979). In 1830, only about 165,000 horsepower were in use, the steam engine capital share was

Table 2.7 Steam's contribution to British labour productivity growth, 1760–1910 (% per year)

	1760–1800	1800–1830	1830–1850	1850–1870	1870–1910
Capital deepening	0.004	0.02	0.16	0.20	0.15
Steam engines	0.004	0.02	0.02	0.06	0.09
Railways			0.14	0.12	0.01
Steamships				0.02	0.05
TFP growth	0.005	0.001	0.04	0.21	0.16
Steam engines	0.005	0.001	0.02	0.06	0.05
Railways			0.02	0.14	0.06
Steamships				0.01	0.05
Total	0.01	0.02	0.20	0.41	0.31

Note: Based on standard neoclassical growth accounting formula disaggregated to include three types of steam capital.
Source: Crafts (2004b).

0.4 per cent and the Domar weight for steam engines was 1.7 per cent (Crafts, 2004a). The cost effectiveness and diffusion of steam power was held back by the high coal consumption of the original low-pressure engines and the move to high pressure – which benefited not only factories but railways and steam ships – was not generally accomplished until the second half of the nineteenth century. The science of the steam engine was not well understood and the price of steam power fell very slowly compared with that of computers in modern times, especially before about 1850. The maximum impact of steam power on British productivity growth was delayed until the third quarter of the nineteenth century – nearly 100 years after James Watt's patent.

2.3   EXPLAINING 'SLOW GROWTH' IN THE FIRST INDUSTRIAL NATION

At a deeper level, it is important to understand why Britain was, in the terms of Figure 1.1, a low λ and low saving economy such that the intersection of the Solow- and Schumpeter-relationship lines was at a fairly low level of technological progress but nevertheless Britain was able to become the Industrial Revolution pioneer. In part, the answer is that British institutions and policies were good by the standards of the time rather than by those of the twentieth or twenty-first centuries. Moreover, it seems that Britain enjoyed transitory advantages conducive to its initial success.

Thus, comparisons of Britain and France from an endogenous-innovation perspective strongly suggest that Britain was much better placed in the late eighteenth century. Despite France's larger population, Britain had access to the largest free trade area in the world and a much better integrated domestic market (Berrill, 1960). Britain was twice as urbanized as France, which reduced the costs of acquiring and developing knowledge (Bairoch, 1991). Britain had a superior expertise in using and assimilating the vital coal-based technologies (Harris, 1976) and there is little doubt that unproductive rent-seeking absorbed far more talent in eighteenth-century France than in Britain (Root, 1991).

Mokyr (2009) develops a similar argument for British primacy. He suggests that what was needed to generate an industrial revolution was the right combination of useful knowledge produced by scientists, engineers and inventors to be exploited by a supply of skilled craftsmen and an institutional environment that provided good incentives for entrepreneurs. Britain was better placed in this regard than any of its Northern European rivals. Central to all this was Britain's embrace of the Enlightenment which promoted both better institutions and an appropriate research agenda whose results were effectively disseminated – in terms of Figure 1.1, a higher λ economy than other late eighteenth-century economies.[2]

Nevertheless, from an endogenous-growth perspective the British economy still had many weaknesses. Accordingly, TFP growth was modest although by the 1830s it was still well ahead of the rate achieved in the United States which averaged 0.2 per cent per year during 1800–1855 (Abramovitz and David, 2001). The size of markets was still very small in 1820 when globalization proper was yet to begin (O'Rourke and Williamson, 2002) and real GDP in Britain was only about 6 per cent of its size in the United States a century later (Maddison, 2010). The costs of invention were high since the contributions that scientific knowledge and formal education could make were modest (Mokyr, 1990). Intellectual property rights were weak since the legal protection offered by patents was doubtful until the 1830s and the cost of taking out a patent was extremely high until 1852 (Dutton, 1984) and the value of patent rights relative to the size of the economy was much smaller than in the twentieth century (Sullivan, 1994). Even if Britain had less rent-seeking than France, rent-seeking in the law, the bureaucracy, the church and the military remained a very attractive alternative to entrepreneurship as the evidence on fortunes bequeathed attests (Rubinstein, 1992).

Obtaining the potential gains from innovation could be problematic, as is reflected by the problems of the textile and engineering

[2]   Crafts (2011) notes that these arguments are attractive but need more quantitative evidence to be fully persuasive.

sectors. In particular, eliciting sufficient effort from the workforce was a significant problem of industrial relations to which solutions had to be devised. In cotton textiles, the answers were found through embracing craft unionism and committing to fixed piecework rates through collective bargaining. This amounted to conceding job control to senior workers and using payment by results rather than managerial authority to underpin the effort bargain. In the short term this delivered higher productivity; for example, the introduction of the 1829 piece-rate list raised labour productivity at M'Connel and Kennedy by 15 per cent (Huberman, 1991). In the longer term, craft control entailed problems of adjusting to changes in circumstances such as new technological opportunities and conflicts related to trials of bargaining strength ensued, notably in engineering highlighted by the famous lockout of the Amalgamated Society of Engineers in 1852 (Burgess, 1975).

Table 2.8 reports levels of investment in physical and human capital in the early nineteenth century which are very low by later standards. This was clearly not a time of high college enrolment and the highly educated were to be found in the old professions not science and engineering. Investment, especially in equipment, was a small proportion of GDP. This may partly reflect the modest capital requirements of the early industrial technologies but is also a symptom of

Table 2.8 *Aspects of broad capital accumulation, 1801–1831 (%)*

Investment/GDP	6.7
Non-residential investment/GDP	5.0
Equipment investment/GDP	1.3
Adult literacy	54
Primary school enrolment	36
Years of schooling (number)	2.0
University students/population	0.04
Civil engineers/employed	0.01
Traditional professions/employed	0.88

Sources: Crafts (1995), (1998) updated for new GDP estimates in Broadberry et al. (2015).

the deficiencies of the capital market at a time of very restrictive company and banking legislation (Harris, 2000). In particular, at times of major government borrowing for military purposes such as during the Napoleonic wars, the Usury Laws meant that the private sector faced severe credit rationing and crowding out (Temin and Voth, 2013).

The limitations of British growth potential at the time of the Industrial Revolution compared with the leading economy 200 years or even 100 years later are reflected in the contributions to productivity growth made by steam in Britain in contrast to electricity and Information and Communication Technology (ICT) in the United States, as reported in Table 2.9. Steam's contribution in Britain was smaller and took much longer to materialize. Indeed, these estimates indicate that already by 2006 the cumulative productivity gain from ICT had matched that of steam over the whole period to 1910. The price of steam power fell much less rapidly than for the more recent technologies implying that rate of improvement of the technology was much slower. It seems reasonable to conclude that over time leading economies have become much better at exploiting general purpose technologies. The reasons are likely to be found in a superior level of education and scientific knowledge, improvements in capital markets, government policies that support research and development, and thus a greater volume of and higher expected returns to innovative effort.

2.4   GETTING AHEAD AND STAYING AHEAD

Britain was well enough served by its institutions and economic policies, was quite capable of developing and investing in new technologies, and achieved leadership in the Industrial Revolution. However, getting ahead was one thing, staying ahead quite another. Over time, growth potential in other countries would improve and the feasible rate of productivity advance would rise markedly as national innovation systems grew stronger. Thus, the advantages identified by Mokyr were temporary, as he stresses (2009, pp. 478–479), and Britain

Table 2.9 *GPTs: contributions to labour productivity growth (% per year)*

Steam (UK)	
1760–1830	0.01
1830–1870	0.30
1870–1910	0.31
Electricity (USA)	
1899–1919	0.40
1919–1929	0.98
ICT (USA)	
1974–1995	0.77
1995–2004	1.50
2004–2012	0.64

Memorandum item: real price falls (%)

Steam horsepower	
1760–1830	39.1
1830–1870	60.8
Electric motors (Sweden)	
1901–1925	38.5
ICT equipment	
1970–1989	80.6
1989–2007	77.5

Notes: Growth accounting contributions include both capital deepening from use and TFP from production.
Price fall for ICT equipment includes computer, software and telecoms; the price of computers alone fell much faster (22.2% per year in the first period and 18.3% per year in the second period).
Sources: Growth accounting: Crafts (2002), (2004a) and Byrne et al. (2013). Price falls: Crafts (2004a), Edquist (2010) and Oulton (2012).

would need to re-invent itself. In time, a different kind of human capital and the educational system to deliver it would be needed to remain a technological leader as formal science came to the fore. Similarly, a more sophisticated capital market, improved intellectual property rights and policies that effectively addressed market failures would have to be introduced. All this is implicit in Table 2.8 which reflects an economy which in terms of Figure 1.1 was, by later standards, both low s and low λ.

The nature of the advantages that underpinned British leadership may actually have been more fragile and transitory than the traditional account recognizes. This would be a corollary of the interpretation of the Industrial Revolution put forward by Allen (2009a) together with related work in the field of 'directed' technological progress. His approach is in the endogenous-innovation tradition and emphasizes the importance of expected profitability to justify the fixed costs of the investment required to perfect good ideas and make them commercially viable. Britain's unique advantages at the time were to be found in the structure of relative prices, characterized by high wages and cheap energy and a sizeable market for the new technologies which initially were profitable to adopt only in these cost conditions. [3]

International comparisons reveal that Britain was an economy that had high wages relative to other countries, a point that has only become firmly established recently, as a result of a long period of successful commercial expansion. Cheap energy was based on the early development of the coal industry, favourable geology and the possibility of transporting coal by water. The rate of return on adopting inventions, and famous inventions in textiles, steam power and coke smelting, was much higher in Britain than elsewhere and so the potential market for these innovations was much greater. As Allen sees it, 'The Industrial Revolution, in short, was invented in Britain in the eighteenth century because it paid to invent it there' (2009a, p. 2). British institutions and policies were adequate for the time but were not markedly superior. Britain did, of course, require an adequate supply of inventors and this may explain why the apparently favourable configurations of relative factor prices which had prevailed in earlier periods did not deliver a pre-Enlightenment Industrial Revolution.

---

[3]   This argument can be given firm theoretical foundations, as Acemoglu (2002) shows.

Allen's interpretation is prima facie plausible and theoretically defensible although more research is required to establish that it stands on really solid empirical foundations (Crafts, 2011). Even so, it is important to recognize that in the context of subsequent relative economic decline and, especially, American overtaking, the suggestion that the key to getting ahead in the Industrial Revolution was relative prices has the clear implication that British leadership was highly vulnerable.

The unique advantage of high wages plus cheap energy was not permanent. First, as the industrial revolution technologies improved, they became profitable to adopt in conditions of lower wages and dearer energy and this allowed other countries to catch up. Second, and more important, insofar as high wages, cheap energy and a market sufficient to allow fixed costs of research and development continued to be conducive to faster technological progress, the United States would be a more favoured location later in the nineteenth century, as has become abundantly clear in the literature on the Habakkuk (1962) hypothesis.

2.5   SOME LEGACIES

Britain's early industrialization was associated with a rather idiosyncratic pattern of development; in a number of ways Britain was an outlier from the 'European Norm' (Crafts, 1984). This is well-known as is the implication that other countries followed different paths to the modern world rather than the British model (O'Brien, 1996). It is much less clear whether the legacy of the early start had adverse effects on later growth performance. This section points to some aspects of the structure of the economy and its institutions which may have mattered and which will be revisited in later chapters.

With regard to economic structure, the obvious starting point is that Britain was an unusually open economy, especially after the move to free trade was completed in the mid-1840s. In 1870, exports of goods and services amounted to 29.1 per cent of GDP (Feinstein, 1972). Britain had a very large share of world manufactured exports – 43 per cent both in 1850 and still in 1875 (Mitchell, 1988). Britain's position in the world economy at the end of the Industrial Revolution entailed exporting a lot of manufactures and importing a substantial amount of agricultural goods. This reflected comparative advantage and was underpinned by technological progress in industry together with diminishing returns in agriculture (Harley and Crafts, 2000).

In 1851, exports accounted for about 25 per cent of industrial gross output and imports supplied around 30 per cent of domestic consumption of agricultural produce (Crafts, 1985, pp. 127, 132). In turn, this configuration of trade patterns was linked to an exceptionally industrialized and non-agricultural employment structure. Table 2.3 reported that, in 1851, 45.6 per cent of the labour force was in industry and only 23.5 per cent in agriculture. The latter figure would not be reached by France and Germany until after the Second World War. The Computable General Equilibrium (CGE) model constructed by Crafts and Harley (2004) explains the small share of employment in agriculture was predicated on an open economy but also reflected to a considerable extent an economy where, unlike in most of Europe, capitalist rather than peasant farming prevailed. The long-run implication of the large weights of exporters of manufactures and of industrial workers who consumed imported food, combined with a low share of agriculture in the economy, was a political bias towards free trade.

Table 2.10 lists the largest 'exports' (positives in the current account) of the British economy in 1870. Several aspects deserve comment, especially in the context of the label, 'workshop of the world'. Cotton and woollen textiles were the leading manufactured exports with £98.1 million compared with £175.4 million for total exports of finished manufactures. Machinery was a relatively small category. In the twentieth century, textiles would be categorized as unskilled-labour intensive goods and, as such, were generally importables for advanced economies as comparative advantage in these items eventually switched to Asia. Across manufacturing sectors as a whole, Crafts and Thomas (1986) found that in 1880 there was

Table 2.10 *Leading positive items in current account of balance of payments, 1870*

	£ million	% total
Services	80.0	22.0
Cotton goods	71.4	19.7
Property income from abroad	37.0	10.2
Woollen goods	26.7	7.4
Iron and steel	23.5	6.5
Coal	5.6	1.5
Machinery	5.3	1.5
Memorandum items		
Visible balance	−33.0	
Invisible balance	88.0	

Source: Mitchell (1988).

a strong correlation between intensive use of relatively unskilled labour and exporting success. This pattern of specialization ultimately entailed major re-adjustments of the labour force as the nineteenth-century export staples declined after the First World War.

A striking feature of the development of industry, and, especially, the export staples, during the period is that there was strong spatial concentration. This was driven in considerable part by factor endowments, notably, the availability of cheap coal which was typically found in the north rather than the south of Britain at least during the Industrial Revolution. Crafts and Mulatu (2006) demonstrated that coal still had a significant influence on industrial location in the late nineteenth century. Mining itself was quite heavily localized with North and Wales representing a third of employment in 1871 rising to 40 per cent by 1911, as is reported in Table 2.11, at which point it accounted for 21 and 25 per cent of employment in these regions, respectively. Shipbuilding and textiles were also highly spatially concentrated and in the latter almost 60 per cent of employment in the sector was in the North West (cottons) and Yorkshire (woollens)

Table 2.11 *Industrial shares of employment* (%)

(a) Share of total industry

	Mining		Ship building		Textiles		All	
	1871	1911	1871	1911	1871	1911	1871	1911
South East	2.17	2.26	19.62	14.17	6.16	6.45	26.19	28.92
East Anglia	0.27	0.21	1.82	0.88	0.97	0.69	3.78	2.72
South West	9.05	3.47	7.68	4.32	3.32	2.10	8.98	6.58
West Midlands	11.38	7.67	1.07	0.36	2.82	2.44	8.44	8.04
East Midlands	7.07	10.15	1.00	0.61	8.00	8.40	6.44	6.66
North West	12.29	10.24	12.69	10.20	38.84	44.49	14.25	15.13
Yorkshire & H	10.24	12.42	3.50	2.90	20.90	20.32	8.62	9.04
North	17.07	19.10	21.34	30.28	1.29	1.24	5.80	6.13
Wales	16.42	20.95	4.82	3.47	0.83	0.94	5.16	5.53
Scotland	14.05	13.53	26.47	32.80	16.88	12.92	12.33	11.25
Britain	100.0	100.0	100.0	100.0	100.0	100.0	100.0	100.0

(b) *Share of regional employment*

	Mining		Ship building		Textiles	
	1871	1911	1871	1911	1871	1911
South East	0.38	0.53	0.39	0.42	2.60	1.84
East Anglia	0.33	0.51	0.25	0.28	2.85	2.10
South West	4.65	3.56	0.44	0.56	4.08	2.64
West Midlands	6.22	6.44	0.07	0.04	3.69	2.51
East Midlands	5.07	10.28	0.08	0.08	13.73	10.40
North West	3.98	4.57	0.46	0.57	30.10	24.26
Yorkshire & H	5.48	9.28	0.21	0.27	26.78	18.56
North	13.58	21.03	1.90	4.22	2.46	1.67
Wales	14.67	25.57	0.48	0.54	1.77	1.41
Scotland	5.26	8.12	1.11	2.49	15.12	9.48
Britain	4.61	6.75	0.52	0.85	11.05	8.25

Source: Lee (1979).

in 1871 at which point 30 per cent of the North West's and 27 per cent of Yorkshire's labour force was in textiles. If globalization went into retreat and/or comparative advantage in these activities ebbed, these regions would be exposed to substantial labour market adjustments.

It is important to recognize the importance of agglomerations both in explaining regional patterns of employment but also in underpinning competitive advantage in international trade. This is epitomized by cotton textiles which became ever more concentrated within a small area centred in Lancashire which accounted for about two thirds of the industry in the mid-nineteenth century and three quarters at the start of the twentieth century. The initial choice of location reflected factors such as the availability of water power and soft water, was refined by focusing on a subset of these locations with cheap coal but then sustained by external economies of scale which accrued through deep labour pools, knowhow and highly specialized suppliers of capital goods, spare parts, marketing etc. (Broadberry and Marrison, 2002). This allowed Lancashire to pay higher wages than elsewhere in the United Kingdom but also to remain internationally competitive at wage rates which were six or seven times those prevailing in Asia (Clark, 1987). As a successful agglomeration, Lancashire dominated export markets far longer than a believer in the Heckscher–Ohlin theory of comparative advantage would have predicted.

The advantages of agglomeration are also central to understanding London's primacy as an international capital market and supplier of internationally traded services which is reflected in the strong contribution already made by 'invisibles' both to the balance of payments overall and in terms of significant exports of services and property income from abroad (Table 2.10). The rise of London to become the largest capital market was driven initially by British economic and commercial success and the blows that the Napoleonic wars delivered to rivals (Cassis, 2006). But its sustained dominance of international financial services was based on input–output linkages within London based on unique advantages in accessing information that accrued to the largest financial centre (Cochrane, 2009). The strength of successful agglomerations such as those in Lancashire and London implied 'crowding out', and it would be harder for new industries to become successful exporters.

The institutional aspects of the industrial revolution economy that both mark Britain out as somewhat unusual and have implications for later growth performance relate to the trajectories on which Britain had embarked in terms of corporate governance and industrial relations which, in the 'Varieties of Capitalism' typology (Hall and Soskice, 2001), would culminate in Britain as a Liberal Market Economy rather than a Coordinated Market Economy.

By the third quarter of the nineteenth century, capital market arrangements had advanced considerably. Hannah (2014) estimated that Britain had a higher ratio of corporate capital to GDP in 1860 (at least 55 per cent) than the United States, France or Germany. The underpinning for a relatively high level of corporatization and shareholding was not only the legislation of the 1850s which allowed joint-stock limited liability companies but also the availability of a wide menu of corporate forms. Banks were relatively unimportant as delegated monitors and Britain was slow to develop investment banking, as might be expected in an economy that was rich by the standards of the time with low interest rates, high levels of private wealth and fairly competitive credit markets (Baliga and Polak, 2004).

There is a considerable contrast with the way in which capital markets would subsequently develop in Germany which came to rely much more on bank than equity finance and indeed on banks that exercised a significant role in control and monitoring of firms (Guinnane, 2002). Once the two finance systems had been established in the context of different initial conditions in terms of the supply of credit, path dependence was not surprising (Baliga and Polak, 2004). The long-term implication for corporate governance was a much greater separation of ownership and control in Britain than in other countries and there were already precursors of this by the late nineteenth century with tendencies to dispersion of share ownership in companies (Acheson et al., 2015) and companies exploiting highly permissive legislation to adopt voting rules that increased the power of directors relative to shareholders (Guinnane et al., 2014).

Britain's relatively small but productive agricultural sector based on capitalist farming reflected the long-standing importance of the market economy (Harley, 2013). Guilds were relatively weak in Britain and had already lost much of their ability to extract rents, enforce apprenticeships and impede the flexibility of production by the early eighteenth century (Daunton, 1995). These institutional arrangements contributed to the emergence of the relatively high incomes which underpinned the incentives to invent industrial revolution technology but also put Britain on an institutional trajectory leading towards the Liberal Market Economy (Iversen and Soskice, 2009).

The implications were a propensity towards craft unionism based on organization of skilled workers and an absence of strong business associations linked to political parties. In turn, this meant an absence of pressure for proportional representation in the electoral system (Cusack et al., 2010). When the franchise became more democratic, the median voter was a skilled worker. Competition for his vote was pursued by both Conservative and Liberal governments which established through the Acts of 1875 and 1906 substantial legal privileges for trade unions whose strategies were to maximize their bargaining power with employers by controlling the supply of skills and content of jobs. The long-term result would see twentieth-century Britain with an industrial relations system based on strong but decentralized collective bargaining (Crouch, 1993).

2.6   CONCLUSIONS

The First Industrial Revolution saw modern economic growth firmly established in Britain. Technological progress accounted for most of the labour productivity growth that permitted the economy to cope with considerable demographic pressure and escape from the Malthusian Trap. Incentives to invest and to innovate were still quite weak by later standards in a context of unsophisticated institutions, small market size, a limited knowledge base and inadequate policies to provide human capital and support research and development. Growth potential was therefore limited and growth performance was modest by later standards. The limitations of the industrial revolution economy are underlined by the very long time that it took to perfect steam technology and for steam to make a serious impact on productivity. To sustain Britain's leadership in future would require further development of growth capabilities.

The early start and the place that it led Britain to occupy in the world economy implied a rather different legacy for future generations compared with other European economies. This entailed precocious industrialization, spatial concentration of economic activity and exports of what would become 'low-tech' manufactures, all of which might lead to difficult adjustment problems. Institutional arrangements implied quite idiosyncratic structures of capital markets and industrial relations. How far all this adversely affected subsequent growth performance will be explored in later chapters.

3   American Overtaking

The leadership of the British economy established during the Industrial Revolution was quite short-lived. By the early twentieth century, although still well ahead of its continental European rivals, Britain had been caught up and overtaken by the United States in terms of real GDP/person (cf. Table 3.1); relative economic decline had started. This does not reflect a decline in British growth potential, which had risen since the Industrial Revolution, but rather a greater increase in productivity growth in the United States associated with the so-called Second Industrial Revolution and a change in the nature of technological progress.

British growth performance in the late nineteenth and early twentieth centuries is controversial. It has frequently been alleged that there was an avoidable failure to exploit the opportunities of the period. Education, industrial relations, management and the capital market have all been criticized. It has been claimed that Britain invested too much abroad and too little at home and was too slow to adopt new technologies and to shift resources into new industries. In all these respects, the United States has been seen as not just different but superior. On the other hand, it might be argued that the United States and Britain had different comparative advantages in international trade, that American factor endowments and geography were more suited to rapid technological advance, that American technology was inappropriate in British cost conditions and that there was nothing that the British business community or policymakers could have done to produce a better outcome.

In this chapter, the well-known debate about 'late Victorian British failure' will be reviewed in the light of recent research and modern growth economics. At the same time, this will allow an

Table 3.1 *Real GDP/person ($1990GK)*

	France	Germany	UK	USA
1870	1876	1839	3190	2445
1899	2911	2905	4567	4051
1913	3485	3648	4921	5301

Source: Maddison (2010).

exploration of the implications of the legacy of the Industrial Revolution. Is this the point at which the 'early start' undermines British economic growth? If so, through what mechanism does this operate – the structure of the economy, constraints on policy or the persistence of institutions?

3.1 A COMPARISON OF BRITISH AND AMERICAN GROWTH PERFORMANCE, 1870–1913

During the late nineteenth and early twentieth century, economic growth in the United States was faster than in Britain and by 1913 the United States had established a clear lead in the level of real GDP per person. Table 3.1 reports the well-known estimates of Maddison (2010), which suggest that the American lead over the United Kingdom in 1913 was about 8 per cent and that overtaking by the United States occurred in the Edwardian period. Recent reworking of the data, in particular to obtain more accurate Purchasing Power Parity (PPP) exchange rates, by Woltjer (2013) indicates that these estimates probably understate relative American performance, such that the United States may have caught Britain up by about 1880 and was about 25 per cent ahead by 1913. It is important to recognize that major European economies, such as France and Germany, did not overtake Britain in this period; on the contrary, Table 3.1 reports that they were still well behind the United Kingdom in 1913, although they had enjoyed some catch-up growth since 1870. Over this period, the French and German growth rates were about 0.5 percentage points higher than Britain, but even so, the gap between French and German levels of real GDP per person and that of the United States widened.

American overtaking was based on superior productivity performance. The estimates reported in Table 3.2 show that labour productivity growth in the United States was superior to that in the United Kingdom across the whole of the private sector during the forty years after 1870. Although much discussion has concentrated on comparisons of manufacturing, we see that the productivity growth gap was much larger in a number of other sectors and superior American performance in services was more important in the overall picture. It should also be noted that, over the period 1871–1911 as a whole, British labour productivity growth was a bit faster than the rate achieved in the first half of the nineteenth century and American outperformance owes much more to acceleration in the United States than slowdown in the United Kingdom.

This point is reinforced by the growth accounting estimates reported in Table 3.3. These show that after the Civil War productivity

Table 3.2 *Sectoral labour productivity growth before the First World War (% per year)*

	UK, 1871–1911	USA, 1869–1909
Agriculture	0.6	1.0
Industry	0.9	1.5
Manufacturing	1.1	1.3
Construction	0.1	2.0
Utilities	1.4	4.0
Services	0.4	1.1
Transport and communications	0.7	2.5
Distribution	−0.3	1.3
Finance and services	0.9	1.4
Government	0.5	0.0
Whole economy	0.8	1.5

Source: Broadberry (2006).

Table 3.3 *Contributions to labour productivity growth (% per year)*

	Education	Capital per hour worked	TFP	Labour productivity growth
United Kingdom				
1856–1873	0.2	0.8	1.2	2.2
1873–1899	0.3	0.4	0.5	1.2
1899–1913	0.3	0.4	−0.2	0.5
1913–1924	0.3	1.3	0.6	2.2
United States				
1800–1855	0.0	0.2	0.2	0.4
1855–1871	0.0	0.5	−0.4	0.1
1871–1890	0.0	0.8	1.0	1.8
1889–1909	0.3	0.5	1.3	2.1

Note: For United Kingdom estimates are for the whole economy and for the USA are for the market sector. Labour productivity growth is measured in terms of GDP per hour worked.
Sources: United Kingdom: Feinstein et al. (1982), Matthews et al. (1982); United States: Abramovitz and David (2001) and Kendrick (1961) with education derived using Morrisson and Murtin (2009) for 1889–1909.

growth in the United States surpassed anything that Britain had achieved during the Industrial Revolution and was far in advance of its own pre-Civil War performance. Initially, this represented post-war recovery but, by the end of the nineteenth century, had moved to a new level in the context of the so-called Second Industrial Revolution. During the early decades of the twentieth century, the United States would be in the forefront of the development of the most important new technologies, including aviation, the internal combustion engine, mass production, electricity and petrochemicals (Mowery and Rosenberg, 2000). This American prowess in technological progress is reflected in Table 3.3 in a significant acceleration in TFP growth to a pace far above that seen in the First Industrial

Revolution.[1] This acceleration was not matched by the United Kingdom and, indeed, TFP growth seems to have been very disappointing in the immediate pre-First World War period, as was stressed by Feinstein et al. (1982), who identified this as a period that could be described as a 'climacteric'.

The notion of a climacteric is of a sharp reduction in trend growth and, as proposed by Feinstein et al. (1982), a cessation of TFP growth between 1899 and 1913. It should be accepted that the existence of a climacteric is not decisive with regard to the growth-failure hypothesis. For example, it has been suggested that a hiatus in British productivity growth resulted from a waning of technological opportunity in a pause between general-purpose technologies with the steam age petering out before the electricity era took over (Lipsey et al., 1998). On the other hand, a constant trend rate of growth could represent a failure if acceleration was possible, as was underlined by Crafts et al. (1989). On balance, however, establishing that there was a climacteric in TFP growth would strengthen the hand of those arguing for a growth failure and would imply that American overtaking owed a good deal to a slowdown in British as well as a speeding up of American growth. So was there a late Victorian/Edwardian climacteric?

Table 3.4 displays the estimates from which Feinstein et al. (1982) inferred a climacteric. They based their analysis on endpoint calculations of growth rates between business-cycle peaks using the 'compromise' measure of GDP, which is a geometric mean of the expenditure, income and output measures.[2] Solomou and Weale (1991) suggested the 'balanced' measure, namely, weighting these alternatives according to their reliability rather than equally, which dilutes the slowdown a bit. The more important point is to note that what Table 3.4 reveals is one

[1] The estimates in Table 3.3 are based on a standard neoclassical methodology as were those of Chapter 2, but are constructed differently in that they do not take account of land inputs and the contribution of education is explicitly recognized. However, this does not undermine the point that TFP growth was clearly much faster in the United States in the early twentieth century than in Britain during the Industrial Revolution.

[2] With fully accurate data each of these measures should give the same GDP estimate, but the quality of the data in this period is imperfect and the discrepancies between the three measures are quite large.

Table 3.4 *Growth of real GDP and TFP, 1856–1937 (% per year)*

	GDP		TFP	
	Compromise	Balanced	Compromise	Balanced
1856–1873	2.2		0.8	
1873–1882	1.9	1.7	0.6	0.4
1882–1889	2.2	1.6	0.9	0.2
1889–1899	2.2	2.2	0.8	0.8
1899–1907	1.2	1.4	-0.3	-0.1
1907–1913	1.6	1.7	0.4	0.5
1924–1929	2.6	2.4	1.2	1.0
1929–1937	2.0	2.0	0.6	0.6

Note: Education included in TFP growth.
Sources: 1856–1913: Compromise estimate from Feinstein et al. (1982)
and balanced estimate from Solomou and Weale (1991); 1924–1937:
Compromise estimate from Matthews et al. (1982) and balanced estimate
from Sefton and Weale (1995).

business cycle with strong growth in the 1890s followed by a very weak
growth cycle between 1899 and 1907 and then a bounceback. This
suggests investigating whether the differences between the various
periods are statistically significant, and it turns out that generally
they are not. A more sophisticated analysis based on time-series econometrics does show a decrease in trend growth after 1899 but of only
about 0.1 percentage points per year (Crafts et al., 1989).

Those who have supported the idea of a climacteric have sometimes supposed that manufacturing productivity growth faltered as
the impetus from steam power waned and old industries, with weak
productivity performance, retained too high a weight in the structure
of the economy. These ideas are misleading, although it is, of course,
true that some steam-intensive sectors such as coal and cotton had
experienced much higher productivity growth earlier in the nineteenth century. Investment in steam power remained very strong as
technological progress continued to reduce its cost, and its contribution to industrial productivity growth peaked in the decades before the

First World War, as can be seen in Table 3.5. Overall, the hypothesis of a serious climacteric is not convincing.

3.2   IMPROVED GROWTH POTENTIAL

The late nineteenth-century British economy clearly had a higher growth potential than had been the case at the time of the Industrial Revolution, and this is reflected in the stronger rate of labour productivity growth – 1.2 per cent per year in 1873–1899 compared with 0.3 per cent per year in 1800–1830 (Tables 2.5 and 3.3). By now, the economy was achieving a higher rate of capital deepening and

Table 3.5 *Steam power growth and British industrial output and labour productivity growth (% per year)*

	1800–1830	1830–1850	1850–1870	1870–1910
Rates of growth				
Steam HP	5.2	5.7	6.3	4.8
Steam HP/worker	2.6	4.1	5.0	3.5
TFP in steam power	0.06	1.2	3.5	1.7
Contributions to output growth				
Steam capital	0.17	0.18	0.35	0.53
TFP in steam power	0.03	0.10	0.13	0.12
Total	0.20	0.28	0.48	0.65
Contributions to labour productivity growth				
Steam capital deepening	0.09	0.13	0.28	0.39
TFP in steam power	0.03	0.10	0.13	0.12
Total	0.12	0.23	0.41	0.51
Memorandum item (%)				
Steam engine income share	3.3	3.2	5.6	11.1

Source: Crafts and Mills (2004).

educational standards were rising quickly. Innovative effort had inten-sified in an economy more conducive to endogenous innovation and TFP growth was more broadly based than during the early nineteenth century. Even so, this was not enough to match the advance in growth potential in the United States, which had moved to a level far ahead of the leader in the First Industrial Revolution.

The simplest measure of the quantity of formal education of the labour force shows a considerable increase so that average years of schooling had advanced from about two years in 1820 to 4.2 in 1870 and 6.75 in 1911 (Morrisson and Murtin, 2009). The quality of educa-tion had also improved, notably in terms of a rapid expansion of scientific and technical education beginning in the late nineteenth century with significant investments in municipal technical colleges, polytechnics and red-brick universities (Sanderson, 1988). Apprenticeship flourished with about 4 per cent of the industrial workforce in this category compared with about 1 per cent a century earlier (Wallis, 2014). Overall, on the eve of the First World War, the British labour force more than matched the United States in terms of skills per worker used in production (Broadberry, 2003).

In the late nineteenth century, capital deepening contributed 0.4 percentage points per year to labour productivity growth. This was higher than at the start of the century partly because the investment rate had risen somewhat (Tables 2.8 and 3.6) and partly because popu-lation growth had slowed down. If all savings had been used at home rather than finding higher returns abroad, the share of investment in GDP would have been some 5 percentage points higher. The capital market had become much more sophisticated; the market value of corporations was 256 per cent of GDP in 1910 (Hannah, 2015) and the stock of corporate bonds had grown to 22 per cent of GDP in 1909 compared with only 0.5 per cent fifty years earlier (Coyle and Turner, 2013). Clearly, further improvements were necessary. For example, company law was inadequate in various respects, which meant com-pany accounts did not present adequate information (Edwards, 1989) and that the market for new issues was inefficient (Foreman-Peck,

1990). Accordingly, an adequate market for corporate control through takeovers did not exist (Hannah, 1974).

TFP growth in the last quarter of the nineteenth century at 0.5 per cent per year was just a little higher than in the first quarter. Nevertheless, it is probably fair to say that the potential for growth based on innovation was stronger than at the time of the Industrial Revolution. In part, this is because TFP growth was less reliant on one star sector, cotton, whose contribution was now much smaller with its TFP growth at about 0.5 per cent per year rather than around 3.5 per cent.[3] In part, incentive structures for endogenous innovation were somewhat more favourable as was reflected in the strength of independent invention under an improved patent system (Nicholas, 2011) and the beginnings of corporate R & D, albeit still on a small scale (Edgerton and Horrocks, 1994). Notably, the greater availability of useful knowledge and trained research personnel allowed science-based technological progress and reduced the costs of innovation (Mokyr, 2002), while the allocation of talent was less distorted as the relative returns to the rent-seeking activities of the early nineteenth century declined.[4]

Nevertheless, in the era of the Second Industrial Revolution, technological leadership moved inexorably to the United States, which exhibited a higher growth potential than contemporaneous or industrial-revolution Britain. Ultimately, the United States made larger investments in advanced human capital and the knowledge economy, which would become central to technological progress in the twentieth century, as is reflected in Table 3.6.

3.3 DID LATE VICTORIAN BRITAIN FAIL?

The heading of this section is also the title of a famous article written by McCloskey. In it he claimed that in the pre-First World War period

---

[3]   This is based on Matthews et al. (1982, pp. 449–450) and the database for Crafts and Mills (2004).

[4]   In 1880, 51.6 per cent of large estates were left by industrialists compared with only 1.9 per cent from the professions and public administration, whereas, in 1809–1839 the percentages were 19.8 from professions and public administration and 9.8 from industrialists (Rubinstein, 1987).

Table 3.6 *The environment for endogenous innovation*

	UK, 1913	USA, 1920
GDP ($1990GK, mn.)	224.6	598.4
Non-residential capital stock ($1990GK, mn.)	301.0	1182.2
Population (mn.)	45.6	106.9
Non-residential investment/GDP (%)	7.4	12.5
R & D expenditure/GDP (%)	0.02	0.25
University students (% population)	0.07	0.56
Civil engineers/employment (%)	0.05	0.13
Traditional professions/employment (%)	0.53	0.95
Years of schooling of labour force	6.47	7.84
TFP growth	0.5	1.4

Note: United Kingdom TFP growth is for 1873–1899 which is regarded as a better reflection of potential than the blip in 1899–1913.
Sources: Crafts (1998) updated, dataset for Broadberry (2006) and Morrisson and Murtin (2009).

the British economy was 'growing as rapidly as permitted by the growth of its resources and the effective exploitation of the available technology' (1970, p. 451). This conclusion was based on three very neoclassical arguments. First, using the insights of the traditional growth model, it was argued that devoting more resources to home investment would have run into diminishing returns. Second, it was claimed that the technical choices made by British firms were efficient and that the highly competitive market environment ensured that there would be no serious and persistent errors at the industry level while the capital market operated to equalize returns at the margin to different types of investment. Third, it was maintained that British productivity growth could not have been any higher. This, in effect, rules out the possibility that the United Kingdom could have anticipated the American move to faster technological change reflected in the TFP growth estimates in Table 3.3.

This assessment has, of course, proved highly controversial and allegations that a number of serious failures, either market failures or government failures, inhibited economic growth have continued. One of the most celebrated of these claims has been 'entrepreneurial failure' (Landes, 1998). Another well-known hypothesis is that the capital market unduly favoured foreign investment and exhibited institutional failures that undermined the flotation of new business and slowed down structural change (Kennedy, 1987). Yet another criticism is that Britain failed to develop the type of national innovation system which would be crucial to twentieth-century economic growth (Goldin and Katz, 2008). Finally, over-reliance on 'self-regulating' markets and a regrettable lack of state intervention was the charge levelled by Elbaum and Lazonick (1986). A notable version of this last argument was made by Richardson (1965), who suggested that tariff protection of new industries was required to prevent an over-reliance on old industries with limited potential for productivity growth.

Some parts of McCloskey's defence of British growth performance stand up well to scrutiny. As Broadberry says, 'In most industries competitive forces acted as a spur to efficiency, with existing rivals or new entrants ready to take up opportunities neglected by incumbent producers' (1997, p. 157). It is a staple of the literature that the only well-established failure to adopt cost-effective new technology, namely, not to switch from the Leblanc to the Solvay process in soda manufacture, was in a cartelized activity, and this is seen as underlining the point that competition was an antidote to entrepreneurial failure (Magee, 2004). In the most-studied choice of technology, that between ring spinning and mule spinning in cotton textiles, the evidence seems clear-cut that the British industry was rational to stick with mule spinning for the vast majority of its production (Ciliberto, 2010; Leunig, 2001). American technology was often not appropriate or lacked technological congruence in British conditions where relative factor prices and market size were different, as Henry Ford found out when trying to use mass-production methods to make cars in Britain.

Although the new economic history has largely succeeded in rejecting claims of managerial failure in the pre-1914 British economy, it is important to recognize that complete exoneration would be going too far. For example, railways was a major sector whose performance was clearly inadequate; Crafts et al. (2008) quantified the excess of actual over minimum feasible costs for a sample of fourteen major railway companies and concluded that median cost inefficiency was 10.2 per cent in 1900, equivalent to about 1 per cent of GDP. Two salient features of the railway sector were that competition was weak and so were shareholders in companies that were notable for the separation of ownership and control. The key point is that this entailed significant principal–agent problems as railway managers had considerable scope to pursue their own objectives and to fail to minimize costs at least while profits remained 'acceptable' (Cain, 1988).[5]

This example should not be taken as typical of the pre-1914 economy; on the contrary, railways were something of an outlier in terms of both barriers to entry and the degree of separation of ownership and control (Cheffins, 2008). However, while railways were the exception in 1900, cases of weak competition together with weak shareholders would become all too common after 1950. So, we may see railways as a harbinger of problems that would impair British economic performance in the decades of acute relative economic decline during the long post-war boom.

It has also become clear that there was no major capital market failure. Foreign investment accounted for about a third of all British savings, but this was justified by the returns available and the diversification of risk that was achieved.[6] British investors would not have been well served by switching out of foreign assets and into new

5   In fact, after 1900, profits became squeezed in the face of regulation of freight charges and rising costs and, as principal-agent models of the firm might predict, managers acted to improve operating efficiency (Irving, 1976); median cost inefficiency in British railway companies fell to 2.6 per cent by 1910 (Crafts et al., 2008).

6   These are the conclusions of two recent studies employing modern portfolio theory. Goetzman and Ukhov (2006) found that diversification permitted a big increase in the Sharpe ratio, while Chabot and Kurz (2010) calculated that the diversification gains were equivalent to a sizeable increase in wealth.

domestic industries (Chabot and Kurz, 2010; Edelstein, 1982). The banking system was not markedly inferior to those of Germany or the United States despite oft-repeated claims to that effect. The British financial system was specialized and the clearing banks provided valuable support to industry through financing working capital while longer term finance could be obtained through corporate bonds and equities and, of course, through retained earnings (Chambers, 2014). Universal banks in Germany did not make a significant difference to the performance of firms with which they had close relationships or supply major amounts of finance for industrialization (Edwards and Ogilvie, 1996; Fohlin, 2012). J. P. Morgan in the United States added value for investors by improving company management and achieving market power through mergers (de Long, 1991) but can hardly be seen as the key underpinning of the acceleration in American TFP growth.

To this extent, McCloskey's position has been vindicated. Yet, it relies fundamentally on the proposition that stronger TFP growth was not possible. Moreover, McCloskey was writing before the advent of endogenous growth economics, which complicates the evaluation of British growth performance. On the one hand, an analysis of this kind might explain the unmatched acceleration of American TFP growth as unavoidable given an economic environment that was more conducive to innovative effort and tended to produce innovations that were unsuited to British conditions. On the other hand, it might point to policy interventions that could have raised British TFP growth but were not pursued.

The estimates in Table 3.7 suggest that the United States had attained a higher TFP level than the United Kingdom by 1911 except in the service sector. The large TFP gap in manufacturing is especially striking, and at first sight this may seem to connote British failure. However, this is probably misleading since these estimates are impacted by the direct impacts of scale economies and natural resources and also by technologies that were developed in the American environment to exploit scale and cheap energy (Abramovitz and David, 2001) but were

Table 3.7 *USA/UK productivity levels in 1911 (UK = 100)*

	Labour productivity	TFP
Agriculture	181	208
Industry	206	161
Manufacturing	214	185
Services	119	79
GDP	138	106

Source: Broadberry (1998) revised in accordance with Woltjer (2013).

not appropriate for British conditions. Cain and Paterson (1986) found that from 1850 to 1920 technological change in American manufacturing generated economies of scale and entailed pervasive materials and capital using and labour saving biases. Moreover, the network of cumulative technological learning was essentially a national one at this time (Nelson and Wright, 1992).[7] In the Second Industrial Revolution this underwrote clear American advantages in much cheaper electricity, which promoted the diffusion of electric motors and the associated transformation of American factories (David, 1991), and in mass production of cars, which was not viable in the much smaller (and more working-class) British market (Bowden, 1991).

In the early twentieth century, the United States had several obvious advantages that endogenous innovation theories might stress because they influenced the expected profitability of costly innovative effort. In the terminology of Figure 1.1, the United States was a relatively high-λ economy. These include a much larger domestic market and capital stock and a greater availability of engineers and science/technology graduates. Large markets encouraged independent inventors (Nicholas, 2010) and partly explain the higher R &

---

[7] This amounts to an argument that technology was not universal. Using this as a defence of McCloskey is somewhat ironic because it is not the standard neoclassical assumption.

D spending of firms in the United States, perhaps 0.25 per cent of GDP (in a much bigger economy) compared with 0.02 per cent in Britain (cf. Table 3.6). American factor endowments encouraged 'directed technical change', which was labour saving and materials using and was often not appropriate for use in British conditions but increased the transatlantic TFP and income gaps. Labour scarcity in the United States may even have increased the rate of technological change (Acemoglu, 2010). These arguments give further reasons to doubt the notion of an avoidable failure.

Unlike later periods, allegations of government failure at this time are about errors of omission rather than commission. The British state continued to have very limited ambitions in terms of economic policy including support for innovation. Although small beginnings were made in promoting scientific research, for example, through the National Physical Laboratory (1899) and the Medical Research Council (1913), public expenditure on science and technology was only 0.06 per cent of GDP in 1914 (Pollard, 1989). This undoubtedly implied that there was too little government support for R & D, a pro-growth activity where social returns exceed private returns. An obvious contrast with the United States was the investment there by state governments in new universities with a greater emphasis on research, professional schools and industrial connections including, notably, MIT (founded in 1862) with its strengths in chemical and electrical engineering (Goldin and Katz, 1999). However, large-scale federal support for R & D in the United States had to await the Second World War (Mowery and Rosenberg, 2000), and the much more important differences between the two countries were in industrial R & D.

3.4 THE 'OVER-COMMITMENT' HYPOTHESIS

Critics of the pre-First World War British economy have frequently argued that while its industrial structure may have reflected comparative advantage in the short run it was not well equipped for long-run productivity growth and, in this regard, compared unfavourably with the United States. The 'old' industries of the First Industrial Revolution were too big and the new industries of the Second Industrial Revolution were too small – for example, too much cotton textiles and too few cars being produced. A very well-known version of this argument was made by Richardson (1965), who claimed that Britain suffered from 'over-commitment' to the old industries and that government should have intervened to speed up the transfer of resources to new industries.

In essence, this is an 'early-start' hypothesis about British relative economic decline in which the market economy was 'locked-in' by its pattern of specialization in international trade to a structure that was suboptimal.[8] It can also be seen as an argument for an 'industrial policy' of the kind which would be adopted in the 1960s and 1970s.[9] In particular, Richardson (1965) suggested that the government should have abandoned free trade and implemented policies of tariff protection for 'infant industries' to facilitate a re-balancing of the economy. The United Kingdom was unusual at this time in its devotion to free trade, despite the presence of a vocal protectionist lobby, partly because the agricultural producer interest was so weak (O'Rourke, 1997), itself a reflection of the early start.

It is certainly the case that Britain's revealed comparative advantage (RCA) looked very different from that of the United States and indeed from what one might expect of an advanced economy of the second half of the twentieth century, as can be seen in Table 3.8. This is reflected, for example, in the rankings of textiles and cars and aircraft. The United Kingdom had a weak position in R & D intensive sectors and the rank correlation of RCA and TFP growth by sector in the

---

[8] A similar argument about industrial structure was made by Kennedy (1987) but on the basis of capital market failure which, as was discussed above, is not very persuasive.

[9] Industrial policy is defined by Warwick (2013), as any type of intervention or government policy that attempts to improve the business environment or to alter the structure of economic activity towards sectors, technologies or tasks that are expected to offer better prospects for economic growth or societal welfare than would occur in the absence of any such intervention.

Table 3.8 *Revealed comparative advantage rankings*

	UK 1913	UK 1937	USA 1913	USA 1937
Agricultural equipment	10	16	2	1
Cars and aircraft	12	11	4	2
Industrial equipment	5	7	3	3
Electricals	8	5	5	4
Iron and steel	3	9	9	5
Non-ferrous metals	16	15	1	6
Book and film	13	8	10	7
Chemicals	11	12	12	8
Metal manufactures	7	13	6	9
Brick and glass	14	10	11	10
Wood and leather	15	14	7	11
Rail and ship	1	3	8	12
Fancy goods	9	4	13	13
Apparel	6	6	14	14
Alcohol and tobacco	4	1	15	15
Textiles	2	2	16	16

Note: Rankings are made on the basis of world market share with 1 = highest.
Source: Crafts (1989).

United States over 1899–1937 was significantly negative (Thomas, 1988). Cotton textiles remained a very strong export with a world market share of about 80 per cent on average during 1880–1911 despite having wage rates which were six times Asian levels because unit costs were held down by the productivity benefits of the Lancashire agglomeration, which had accrued from the early start (Crafts and Leunig, 2005).

Nevertheless, this 'over-committed' structure did not entail a productivity growth penalty before the First World War. Table 3.9 reports a calculation of the difference that United Kingdom (rather than American) employment shares would have made to overall American labour productivity growth in manufacturing assuming that sectoral productivity levels and growth rates remained unchanged. The difference is trivial but actually goes in the direction of *raising*

Table 3.9 *Impact of changing sectoral weights on labour productivity growth in US manufacturing, 1899–1909 (% per year)*

USA weights	1.65
UK weights	1.73
Post-tariff UK weights	1.76

Note: Calculations based on fixed 1900 weights in each case where the weight for sector i uses the formula in Nordhaus (1972) and is $[(Y/L)_i/(Y/L)_{manf}]s_i$ where Y/L is labour productivity and s is the share of manufacturing employment. In each case the term in square brackets is based on productivity data for the United States and the employment shares are as follows: row 1 is actual United States in 1900, row 2 is actual United Kingdom in 1907 and row 3 is counterfactual United Kingdom with Chamberlain tariff in 1907.
Sources: Derived from Kendrick (1961), Niemi (1974) and Thomas (1984).

American productivity growth. If productivity growth was disappointing in British manufacturing in the Edwardian period, this was a problem of within-sector performance not composition of activity.

It is well-known that, although Britain maintained policies of free trade, the United States was a high-tariff country with an average tariff rate on manufactures of around 40 per cent. This does not mean, however, that American overtaking was the result of protectionism. Irwin (2001) pointed out that faster productivity growth in the United States mainly accrued in non-traded sectors (cf. Table 3.2) which did not benefit from protection and that American policies did not add up to a successful infant-industry strategy. More generally, careful econometric analysis of the cross-country evidence does not support the hypothesis that higher tariffs raised growth rates in this period – if anything it points to the opposite conclusion (Schularick and Solomou, 2011). This may reflect the tendency for protection not to be tightly focused on a few selected sectors with excellent growth prospects or positive externalities for the rest of the economy (Tena-Junguito, 2010).

Similar problems would surely have undermined any British attempt to use protectionism to promote faster growth. The political economy of tariff protection was such that the proposals that had the most political support such as those made by Chamberlain would have actually tended to divert employment towards traditional sectors such as agriculture and textiles, which were relatively labour intensive rather than new growth industries (Thomas, 1984).[10] A general tariff policy would have weakened competition in product markets with potentially adverse effects on productivity performance. In any case, if the real problem was market failures that implied too little investment in human capital and R & D, then the right response was policy intervention by government to address these failures directly.

3.5 INSTITUTIONAL TRAJECTORIES

As Chapter 2 highlighted, there were important institutional legacies of the Industrial Revolution, especially with regard to corporate governance and industrial relations, which had the potential to affect subsequent economic performance. At this point, it is opportune to review the state of play in these areas in the early twentieth century. The picture that emerges is that Britain had moved further down the paths which were already mapped out in the mid-nineteenth century.

With regard to corporate governance, equity finance of joint-stock limited liability companies had been embraced on quite a wide scale despite the very weak levels of shareholder protection provided

---

[10]   Thomas (1984) estimated that employment in agriculture and textiles would have risen by 45441 and 149851, respectively, while employment in chemicals, motor and cycle and engineering would have risen by 241, 3102 and 10619, respectively, had a Chamberlain tariff been introduced in 1907 reflecting the pattern of effective protection that this would have entailed. As Table 3.9 reports, the difference to productivity growth implied by the reweighting of sectors would probably have been small. When tariffs were introduced in interwar Britain, the largest increases in effective rates of protection went to 'old' industries such as hosiery and lace and railway rolling stock (Kitson et al., 1991), which was hardly a well-targeted infant-industry approach.

by company law. Recent research has established that many companies had diffuse share ownership and it is possible already to see
a significant separation of ownership and control. For example,
Acheson et al. (2015) found that in companies registered between
1881 and 1902 the median holding of the largest shareholder and the
directors was 6.4 and 9.0 per cent of the capital, respectively. For very
large companies in 1911, Foreman-Peck and Hannah (2012) found that
the median value of shares held by the directors was only 2.4 per cent.
That said, it was possible for control in voting rights to stay quite
tightly held in many companies whose shares were traded on the stock
exchange; for Initial Public Offering (IPO)s between 1900 and 1911,
insiders on average controlled over 55 per cent of voting rights and
dispersion of initial holdings was fairly slow (Cheffins et al., 2013).

It seems clear that the principal–agent problems of the railways,
which stemmed from very weak shareholders and barriers to entry,
were not typical of this period. Foreman-Peck and Hannah (2013)
found no evidence that diffuse shareholding in large companies was
associated with under-performance in terms of profitability while
managerial discipline together with shareholder protection seems to
have been underpinned by high levels of dividend payouts (Campbell
and Turner, 2011). Shares were still nearly always held by individuals,
many of whom lived locally, rather than institutions while coalitions
of a relatively small number of shareholders may have sufficed to
provide an important check on managers.[11] At the same time, the
way was open for a future evolution towards a much more problematic
separation of ownership and control later on.

By the early twentieth century the British system of industrial
relations had developed considerably from the Industrial Revolution
era but retained distinctive features inherited from the mid-
nineteenth century. Many more workers were members of trade

---

[11] In a sample drawn from public companies in 1920, on average, the nine largest shareholders owned 50 per cent of the voting rights (Franks et al., 2009). By contrast, the
largest railway companies had over 70,000 shareholders in 1911 (Foreman-Peck and
Hannah, 2012).

unions – almost 25 per cent of the labour force in 1913 compared with 4 per cent as recently as 1890 – and collective bargaining over wages had become quite widespread – 2.4 million workers covered by such agreements in 1910 (Aldcroft and Oliver, 2000). By then trade union-ism was spreading to unskilled workers, but its defining characteristic remained craft unionism. So in many important industries multi-unionism prevailed and the typical union represented a small subset of the workforce. Despite the founding of the Trade Union Congress (TUC) in 1868, industrial relations remained decentralized.

The continued strength of craft unionism entailed craft control of work on the shop floor and the use of piece rates to elicit effort. This had emerged as a solution to appropriation problems during the Industrial Revolution and was still the preferred management style of many British employers, at least partly because they perceived the 'switching costs' of imposing greater direct managerial control as too high. There were periodic disputes over the details of these arrange-ments, including, most notably, the engineering lockout of 1897/1898, but, in the aftermath, employers did not seek to end craft control on this and other occasions when they 'won' the dispute.[12] Arguably, these institutional arrangements served Britain well through the nine-teenth century (Lazonick, 1994). When, however, the Fordist technol-ogies of the Second Industrial Revolution came along with requirements for large sunk-cost investments in fixed capital, firms were inhibited from adopting them by exposure to 'hold-up' problems. Unions lacked an ability to commit to cooperative behaviour and the effort levels required, for example, by mass production methods in the car industry (Lewchuk, 1987).

Together with the expansion of the franchise in 1867 and 1884, the value that employers placed on Victorian industrial relations informed the legal privileges given to trade unions in the 1906 Trade Disputes Act, which granted complete legal immunity to trade unions from all actions at tort and went beyond the already extensive

[12] In contrast with their American counterparts who had more to gain from eliminating craft control (Haydu, 1988).

immunities thought to have been granted in 1875 (Phelps Brown, 1983).[13] This gave trade unions considerably enhanced bargaining power and remained essentially unreformed for over sixty years.

The strength of craft unionism in Britain may also have had political consequences by precluding a move to proportional representation. Cusack et al. (2007, 2010) argue that its presence meant that there was no incentive to move away from a majoritarian system of voting in an economy where there was no prospect of gains for the right from collective institutions to deliver investment in skills. And, if winning elections meant wooing the median voter who was a skilled worker, in turn this underpinned craft unionism, as 1906 underlined. Thus, an equilibrium was sustained that mitigated against moving towards a coordinated market economy.

3.6 CONCLUSIONS

Overall, it seems reasonable to conclude that there was no massive growth failure in the pre-1914 economy. Any decline in the trend growth rate was slight and American outperformance probably had its roots in unique American advantages based on a favourable configuration of factor endowments and market size, rather than serious errors by British business or governments. That said, the neoclassical exoneration of British performance epitomized in the title of the well-known survey article by McCloskey and Sandberg (1971) surely went too far, as is illustrated by the example of the railways. Arguably, also British governments might have done more to establish a stronger national innovation system.

There is also no strong argument that the early start was a serious handicap on British growth performance in the decades before the First World War. Certainly, British comparative advantage was still concentrated in the 'old' nineteenth-century industries, but this structure was not yet a big disadvantage; American

---

[13] Contrary to the intentions of the 1875 legislation, the House of Lords had in 1901 ruled in favour of the Taff Vale Railway Company and awarded damages against the Amalgamated Society of Railway Servants which had organized a strike.

outperformance was intra-sectoral and in services. Early industrialization and the strength of London as a financial centre meant that Britain was an enthusiastic participant in the globalizing economy, but policies of openness served the economy well both in capital and product markets. The early start mitigated against protectionist policies, but this did not entail a pre-1914 growth penalty, although it increased the economy's exposure to globalization risks and future adjustment problems.

The institutional legacies of the early start were apparent in terms of idiosyncratic industrial relations and corporate governance. This was apparent in the strength of craft unionism and a precocious separation of ownership and control. These configurations had potential downsides in terms of the diffusion of the technologies of the Second Industrial Revolution and scope for managerial failures, but any adverse impact on economic performance lay mainly in the future.

4 The Interwar Years: Onwards and Downwards

The year 1913 was the end of an era; during the following 25 years the economy operated in a very different environment subjected to massive shocks and a new political climate. Successive blows came with the First World War, the Great Depression and a reversal of the globalization process which had defined the period from the mid-nineteenth to the early twentieth century. The extension of the franchise was accompanied by a new competition for votes of workers and of women, together with the demise of the Liberal Party. The electorate in the 1929 election when the Labour Party won 37 per cent of the votes and 47 per cent of the seats, was about 29 million compared with 7.7 million in 1910 (Middleton, 1996).

The adjustment problems arising from these changed circumstances were severe. They included dealing with a greatly increased national debt, coping with structural unemployment, arriving at a new macroeconomic policy framework and addressing the difficulties of the Victorian export industries. The implication was a transformation of the policy landscape; by the 1930s laissez faire had been replaced by the 'managed economy' (Booth, 1987). The gold standard and free trade had been superseded by a managed floating exchange rate and a general tariff on manufactures, taxation was a much higher share of GDP, unemployment benefits had replaced the Poor Law and industrial policy had been introduced.

Not surprisingly, perhaps, traditional views of interwar economic performance were pessimistic. Nevertheless, between the peak years of 1924 and 1937 both output and labour inputs grew only marginally more slowly than between 1873 and 1913 (Matthews et al., 1982, p. 208). Indeed, following a lengthy discussion of British performance, textbook accounts became quite optimistic:

'The view that, after a poor performance in the 1920s, the 1930s saw a genuine breakthrough, is indeed widespread and finds support not only in the output statistics but also in the quality of the modern investment and structuring of British industry towards the growth-oriented sectors...' (Pollard, 1992, p. 39). This relatively favourable interpretation appears to be echoed by the emphasis placed by Matthews et al. (1982, pp. 506–507) on a U-shaped pattern in TFP growth with a low in the early twentieth century, followed by a revival in the interwar period, leading on to an all-time high after the Second World War. It should be noted, however, that these accounts lack an adequate comparative perspective.

This discussion raises a number of questions which are the focus of this chapter. How impressive was growth performance? What part did 'new industries' play in growth outcomes? Did the new supply-side policy have positive effects? Were problems of the early start now over?

4.1 GROWTH PERFORMANCE AND POTENTIAL

At the end of the interwar period, the United Kingdom's lead over France and Germany in terms of real GDP per person was quite similar to that of 1913 according to the estimates by Maddison (2010) reported in Table 4.1. Making comparisons vis-à-vis the United States is a bit more complicated. The estimates in Table 4.1 show a widening of the gap between 1913 and 1929 from under 8 per cent to about 25 per cent followed by a substantial narrowing to about 3 per cent in 1937. Prima

Table 4.1 *Real GDP/person ($GK1990)*

	France	Germany	UK	USA
1913	3485	3648	4921	5301
1929	4710	4051	5503	6899
1937	4487	4685	6218	6430

Note: United States in 1941 = $8206
Source: Maddison (2010).

facie, this seems to show a significant catching up and reversal of relative economic decline by Britain during the depression years of the 1930s. This is, however, rather misleading for several reasons.

First, the choice of the end year in Table 4.1 favours the United Kingdom. By 1937, the business cycle recovery from the shock of the Great Depression was complete whereas, in the United States this took until 1941. In 1941, real GDP per person in the United States was $8206 (1990$GK); over a twelve-year cycle it had grown on average by 1.46 per cent per year compared with 1.55 per cent over the eight-year cycle in the United Kingdom between 1929 and 1937. It may be better to see the Great Depression and its aftermath, as a phase where relative economic decline paused rather than was reversed, even though the United States experienced by far the bigger trauma. Second, the transatlantic income gap may be underestimated in Table 4.1. Using the PPP exchange rates calculated by Woltjer (2013), the income gap between Britain and the United States had widened from about 25 per cent in 1913 to about 40 per cent by 1929. Third, on the other hand, the widening of the gap between the two countries between 1913 and 1929 exaggerates the difference in underlying trend growth potential because the shock of the First World War had an adverse impact on income levels in 1920s' Britain by raising (equilibrium) unemployment and reducing trade exposure through increasing trade costs. This was equivalent to a levels shock to GDP of perhaps 7.5 per cent (Crafts, 2014).

Growth accounting estimates reported in Table 4.2 show that productivity growth in the United Kingdom continued to be well below that of the United States. There was a revival compared with the very disappointing outcome for 1899–1913 but during 1924–1937 labour productivity growth and TFP growth were below the levels of 1873–1899. In sharp contrast, TFP growth in the United States rose to new heights which were sustained through the 1930s, described by Field (2011) as America's 'most technologically progressive decade of the twentieth century'. The revival of TFP growth stressed by Matthews et al. (1982) is more apparent at a disaggregated level, as

Table 4.2 *Contributions to labour productivity growth (% per year)*

	Education	Capital per hour worked	TFP	Labour productivity growth
UK				
1924–1937	0.3	0.1	0.3	0.7
USA				
1919–1929	0.3	0.3	1.8	2.4
1929–1941	0.3	0.1	2.1	2.5

Note: Estimates for United States are for the private domestic economy.
Sources: Matthews et al. (1982); Kendrick (1961) and education
contributions derived from Morrisson and Murtin (2009).

Table 4.3 *Crude TFP growth in major sectors (% per year)*

	UK, 1873–1913	UK, 1924–1937	USA, 1919–1941
Agriculture	0.4	2.1	2.1
Mining	–0.1	1.2	2.7
Manufacturing	0.6	1.9	3.8
Construction	0.1	1.3	0.7
Utilities	1.6	1.8	3.9
Transport and communications	0.7	1.0	3.1
Commerce	0.5	–0.5	1.1
GDP	0.4	0.7	2.2

Note: Crude TFP means that labour quality (education) is not separately
accounted for.
Sources: Update of Kendrick (1961) in Bakker et al. (2017); Matthews,
Feinstein and Odling-Smee (1982.)

can be seen in Table 4.3, where most sectors, notably including manufacturing, achieved much stronger TFP growth in 1924–1937 than in
1873–1913. The big exception to this was 'commerce' (distribution,

finance and miscellaneous services) which detracted significantly from overall TFP growth. Poor performance in commerce may have reflected disguised unemployment in hard times. Again, however, in most sectors, including manufacturing, interwar-period British TFP growth was well below the American level.

The United Kingdom struggled to match American productivity performance in the industries at the heart of the Second Industrial Revolution. Comparing Britain in 1924–1937 with the United States in 1919–1941, crude TFP growth in vehicles/transport equipment was 3.1 per cent per year compared with 6.5 per cent, in electrical engineering/electric machinery it was 2.0 per cent compared with 5.0 per cent, and in chemicals 1.4 per cent compared with 4.1 per cent. In particular, Britain was much less well placed than the United States to benefit from the new general purpose technology, electricity. As electrical power became a cheap input in the United States and there was a rapid shift to machinery powered by unit drive, factory design became much more flexible and capital-saving improvements were developed (David, 1991). More than 20 per cent of TFP growth in American manufacturing in the 1920s derived from these spillover effects (Bakker et al., 2017). Electricity consumption per employee in manufacturing in the United States was more than three times the British level in 1930 when the British price was about 50 per cent higher; there was no strong impact of electrical power on British manufacturing productivity (Ristuccia and Solomou, 2014).

By the 1930s, underlying growth potential in the United Kingdom was somewhat higher than in 1913 on account of greater investments in human capital and R & D, as is reflected in Table 4.4. Both government and industry spent increasing amounts on R & D and employment in industrial R & D was in excess of 4,000 by 1938 when, however, the comparable figure for the United States was above 44,000 (Edgerton and Horrocks, 1994). Years of schooling continued to increase and had reached 7.5 years by the late 1930s. Here also, the United States had pulled further ahead especially in terms of post-14 education. By 1938, 45 per cent of 17 year olds were high-school graduates in the United States, whereas only 4 per cent of British 17-year olds were in school

Table 4.4 *Investments in broad capital*

	UK, 1937	USA, 1940
Non-residential investment (%GDP)	6.4	7.6
Years of schooling, ages 15–64	7.5	8.8
R & D expenditure (%GDP)	0.4	0.7

Sources: Non-residential investment: Feinstein (1972), Carter et al. (2006); Years of schooling: Morrisson and Murtin (2009); R & D (for 1934): Edgerton (1996).

(Goldin and Katz, 2008) and average years of tertiary education were in the United States about three times the British level (Broadberry, 2003).[1] Although, in the terminology of Figure 1.1, the United Kingdom was now a somewhat higher-λ economy than at the end of the nineteenth century, it still compared quite unfavourably with the United States.

4.2 THE INTERWAR UNEMPLOYMENT PROBLEM

The defining feature of the interwar British economy was persistently high unemployment. As measured by the unemployment rate of workers enrolled in the national insurance scheme, unemployment was only below 10 per cent in one year (9.7 per cent in 1927), averaged 14.2 per cent over 1921–1938, and peaked at 22.1 per cent in 1932 during the Great Depression. The unemployment rate for the whole labour force was lower but nevertheless averaged 10.9 per cent, nearly twice the 5.8 per cent average for 1870–1913 (Boyer and Hatton, 2002).

These averages mask considerable variations not only between years of recession and recovery but also, strikingly, between industries and regions, as is reported in Table 4.5. Relatively high rates of unemployment were experienced in 'outer Britain' and in the Victorian staple industries compared with 'inner Britain' and the new industries of the Second Industrial Revolution. High regional unemployment was associated with the spatial concentration of activities such as

---

[1] Taking the average of estimates for 1913 and 1950 for ages 15–64 reported by Broadberry (2003) gives 0.10 years for the United Kingdom and 0.32 years for the USA.

Table 4.5 *Unemployment rates (%)*

	1924	1929	1932	1937
Coalmining	5.8	19.0	34.5	16.1
Cotton textiles	15.9	12.9	30.6	10.9
Iron and steel	22.0	20.1	47.9	11.4
Shipbuilding	30.3	25.3	62.0	24.4
Woollen textiles	8.4	15.5	22.4	8.8
Cars and aircraft	8.9	7.1	22.4	5.0
Chemicals	9.9	6.5	17.3	6.8
Electrical engineering	5.5	4.6	16.8	3.1
London	9.0	5.6	13.5	6.4
South East	7.5	5.6	14.3	6.7
South West	9.1	8.1	17.1	7.8
Midlands	9.0	9.3	20.1	7.3
North West	12.9	13.3	25.8	14.0
North East	10.9	13.7	28.5	11.1
Wales	8.6	19.3	36.5	23.3
Scotland	12.4	12.1	27.7	16.0
UK insured workers	10.3	10.4	22.1	10.8
UK all workers	7.9	8.0	17.0	8.5

Note: All estimates are for insured workers except bottom row.
Sources: Garside (1990) and Boyer and Hatton (2002).

coalmining and textiles but in the worst affected areas unemployment was higher across all sectors. In February 1938, 20.5 per cent of male applicants for unemployment benefit had been unemployed for 12 months or more compared with 10.7 per cent in 1929 (Crafts, 1987). Long-term unemployment was concentrated in 'outer Britain' especially among older workers. Whereas 5.8 per cent of male claimants had been out of work for over a year in London at this time, the corresponding figure for Wales was 30.7 per cent, and for male workers aged 45–64 in Wales, 45.8 per cent. Overwhelmingly, contemporaries saw this as an 'industrial problem' which inflicted severe welfare losses on those trapped in this state (Pilgrim Trust, 1938).

The legacy of nineteenth-century industrialization in a free-trade economy left Britain exposed to high unemployment risks and significant labour-market adjustment problems. Trade wars and the world economic downturn severely affected 'outer Britain'. Employment in coalmining, shipbuilding and textiles fell by 741,000 between the Censuses of Production in 1924 and 1935, and around half of this decline can be attributed to falls in exports. The structure of employment in the South East, and to a lesser extent the West Midlands, was skewed towards expanding sectors while declining sectors loomed large in the North East, North West and Wales. Shift-share analysis confirms that structural differences accounted for most of the large gap in employment growth between these regions during the interwar period (BPP, 1940). The South East (Greater London) secured 47.9 per cent (39.6 per cent) of new manufacturing plants during 1932–1938 (Scott and Walsh, 2005). In a new environment of electrical power and road haulage, the advantages of proximity to markets implied different industrial location decisions and that the employment geography of Victorian Britain had become outdated. Electrical engineering and the car industry preferred the South East and the West Midlands to the North East and Wales. Spatial as well as structural adjustment was required.

Not only was the actual rate of unemployment higher in the interwar period than before the First World War but so too was the Non-accelerating Inflation Rate of Unemployment (NAIRU). Hatton and Thomas (2013) estimate that it had increased from 5.7 per cent in 1891–1913 to 9.5 per cent in 1921–1938. Besides the structural problems of the staple industries, U^* rose in response to the spread of collective bargaining and the introduction of unemployment insurance which reduced the flexibility of the labour market, especially in responding to adverse shocks. These changes can be understood as further consequences of competition for working class votes. The implication was that reform of the labour market was required if unemployment was to return to lower levels on a sustainable basis; a 'Keynesian solution' based on stimulating aggregate demand would be inadequate, notwithstanding the positive effects of rearmament in reducing unemployment in the later 1930s.[2]

The intractability of the interwar unemployment problem had its roots in the industrial legacy of the early start. Persistent unemployment was an 'inescapable experience' for a generation of politicians who would make economic policy after the Second World War, and provoked a strong reaction against the market economy and in favour of much greater government intervention that would have been inconceivable a quarter of a century earlier, as is reflected, for example, by the case of Harold Macmillan, a Conservative who would become Prime Minister in 1957 but was MP for Stockton-on-Tees in the 1930s (Macmillan, 1938).

4.3   THE 1930S: ECONOMIC RENAISSANCE?

If the economy was regenerated between the wars, it might seem natural to expect that structural change played a large part, and this was central to the controversial interpretation put forward by Richardson (1967) which stressed the end of over-commitment and the contribution of 'new industries' to productivity growth. A 'new industries' interpretation of interwar growth is not necessary for claims that productivity performance improved but it might seem to add to their plausibility.

Table 4.6 reports on the extent to which 'new industries' were responsible for the growth of labour productivity between the Census of Production years of 1924 and 1935 using the widest available definition of the term. Since, on average, they represented about 6 per cent of

---

[2]   It quickly became Keynesian orthodoxy that rearmament had made a big contribution to cutting unemployment. Bretherton et al. (1941) estimated that unemployment in 1938 would have been 1.2 million higher in the absence of rearmament. Later estimates by Thomas (1983) reduced this impact to about 1million (with an addition of about 6 per cent to GDP) based on a government-expenditure multiplier of 1.6. More recent research by Crafts and Mills (2013) suggests that the multiplier was no more than 0.8 and that Thomas' estimates are about twice the true impact.

Table 4.6 *Sectoral contributions to manufacturing labour productivity growth (%)*

	Growth, 1924–1935	1924 weight	Share	1935 weight	Share
New industries					
Motor and cycle	4.6	3.8	10.11	5.1	12.67
Silk and artificial silk	8.7	0.9	4.53	1.1	5.17
Chemicals	2.4	2.8	3.89	3.9	5.12
Rubber	7.6	1.0	4.43	1.2	4.96
Paper and printing	1.7	4.2	3.75	4.4	4.01
Electrical engineering	0.9	2.8	1.52	4.6	2.34
Aircraft	3.4	0.2	0.40	0.7	1.30
Scientific instruments	3.0	0.4	0.70	0.5	0.82
Aluminium, lead, tin	1.5	0.5	0.43	0.8	0.64
Petroleum	4.3	0.2	0.56	0.2	0.50
Total	*3.1*	*17.0*	*30.32*	*22.5*	*37.51*
Old staples					
Mechanical engineering	1.4	7.3	5.93	7.7	5.83
Iron and steel	1.8	5.5	6.05	5.7	5.57
Clothing	1.1	8.0	5.74	7.9	4.90
Woollens and worsted	1.9	4.5	5.01	3.5	3.64
Cotton spinning and weaving	1.6	7.1	6.91	3.2	2.79
Other textiles	1.2	4.1	3.46	3.0	1.89
Timber	1.3	0.8	0.61	1.1	0.79
Furniture	0.7	1.2	0.51	1.6	0.63
Leather etc.	1.0	1.0	0.54	0.8	0.42
China and earthenware	0.5	0.9	0.28	0.7	0.19
Rope, twine and net	1.6	0.2	0.19	0.2	0.17
Shipbuilding	0.1	2.1	0.13	1.2	0.07
Railway carriage	0.2	0.5	0.05	0.4	0.04
Total	*1.3*	*43.4*	*35.41*	*37.0*	*26.93*

Source: Broadberry and Crafts (1990).

total employment; their impact in raising the growth of labour productivity could not have been dramatic. There is no reason to think
that the contribution of the new industries was particularly special.
In any dynamic economy, it is normal for newer industries to grow
faster than mature sectors. Clearly, 'new industries' more than
punched their weight, especially if the calculation is based on 1935
value-added shares, in terms of their impact through intra-sectoral
productivity growth. On the other hand, a calculation of their impact
through structural change shows that this was very small; productivity growth took place overwhelmingly within sectors rather than
through shifts of resources between sectors and, in any case, structural
change was relatively slow (Matthews et al., 1982).[3]

Again it is helpful to place the productivity performance of the
new industries in an international perspective. Here, two points stand
out. First, in most cases labour productivity was further behind the
United States than the average for all manufacturing where the USA/
UK ratio of real value added per worker in 1935 was 2.24. In chemicals,
the ratio was 2.69, in electrical engineering 3.18, in motor vehicles
4.62 (de Jong and Woltjer, 2011). Second, the new industries did not
establish a strong position in terms of revealed comparative advantage
in exporting, where the most notable feature of the late 1930s was the
persistence of the old staples as the United Kingdom's strongest export
sectors (cf. Table 3.8). These comparisons rather temper enthusiasm
about the performance of the new industries.

More generally, it is difficult to accept the suggestion that there
was a marked improvement in British growth performance in the
1930s, although there were some positive signs. As is reported in
Table 4.4, non-residential investment as a share of GDP was only
6.4 per cent in the 1930s, although R & D rose to 0.4 per cent of
GDP. Crude TFP growth averaged 0.6 per cent per year in 1929–1937
compared with 0.7 per cent in 1873–1899 (Feinstein et al., 1982;

[3]   Using a standard decomposition based on Nordhaus (1972), Broadberry and Crafts
(1990) reported that structural change added 0.02 percentage points to manufacturing
productivity growth between 1924 and 1935.

Table 4.7 *Real output/hour worked in manufacturing*

	UK growth (% per year)	US growth (% per year)		US/UK (UK = 100)
			1870	195.2
1870–1890	1.58	1.75	1890	201.9
1890–1913	1.33	2.11	1913	241.2
1913–1929	2.46	3.05	1929	264.5
1929–1937	2.90	3.35	1937	274.0

Source: de Jong and Woltjer (2011); data kindly supplied by Herman de Jong.

Matthews et al., 1982). The 1930s did see a strong recovery in GDP after 1933 but, considering the post-1929 business cycle as a whole there is no sign of a trend break in the growth of either GDP or industrial production (Mills, 1991; Greasley and Oxley, 1996). Labour productivity growth in manufacturing was much stronger in the 1930s than before 1913, as Table 4.7 reports, but that table also shows output per hour worked continued to grow faster in United States manufacturing, so that the level of American labour productivity was 2.74 times that of the United Kingdom in 1937 compared with 2.41 in 1913 and 2.64 in 1929.

It is, of course, true that the British economy experienced several years of very strong growth in the aftermath of the severe recession of the early 1930s. From 1933 to 1937, real GDP grew by at least 3.1 per cent each year and in total the economy expanded by almost 20 per cent. This should, however, be seen as a cyclical recovery driven by demand rather than as a change in trend growth. The impetus came from a big reduction in real interest rates under the 'cheap money policy' adopted in 1932 after the United Kingdom had left the gold standard, subsequently boosted by a fiscal stimulus from rearmament after 1935 (Crafts, 2013).

From 1932, there was coherence in the Treasury's thinking which deserved the label of a 'managed-economy' approach (Booth, 1987). The central objective was a steady increase in the price level – which on the assumption that money wages would not react also amounted to reducing real wages and restoring profits – subject to not letting inflation spiral out of control. The Chancellor of the Exchequer announced the objective of raising prices in July 1932 and subsequently reiterated it frequently. The rise in the price level was promoted through cheap money, a weak pound, tariffs and encouraging firms to exploit their (enhanced) market power. This strategy was clearly quite similar to a price-level target to increase the expected rate of inflation and reduce real interest rates, even at the lower bound for nominal interest rates. Obviously, this strategy does not represent an irrevocable commitment but it was a credible policy given that the Treasury and the Chancellor of the Exchequer were in charge.[4] Cheap money and a rise in the price level were clearly in the Treasury's interests from 1932 as a route to recovery, better fiscal arithmetic and to provide an alternative to the Pandora's Box of jettisoning balanced-budget orthodoxy and adopting Keynesianism (Howson, 1975).

The managed-economy framework successfully promoted recovery but at the cost of a serious retreat from competition in product markets. The interwar economy exhibits symptoms of a considerable increase in market power. By 1935, the share of the largest 100 firms in manufacturing output had risen to 23 per cent following a merger boom in the 1920s; growing industrial concentration and increased barriers to foreign entry greatly strengthened domestic cartels (Hannah, 1983). Mercer (1995) showed that by 1935 at least 29 per cent of manufacturing output was cartelized. A proxy for the price-cost margin [(value-added – wages)/value added] calculated from the Census of Production shows an average increase of 3.8 percentage points across all manufacturing sectors from 1924 to 1935 while in the sectors identified by Mercer as cartelized the increase was 9.0 percentage points. Hart (1968) estimated that the

---

[4]   This would not have been the case had the Bank of England run monetary policy. Governor Norman plainly disliked cheap money and regarded it as a temporary expedient (Howson, 1975, p. 95).

rate of return on capital employed for manufacturing companies had risen to 16.2 per cent by 1937 from 11.4 per cent in 1924.

There is, however, no evidence that the retreat from competition in the 1930s was good for productivity performance; if anything, the opposite is the case. Broadberry and Crafts (1992) examined the impact of reduced competition on productivity. Controlling for other variables, they found a negative correlation between changes in the price-cost margin and productivity performance for a cross-section of British industries in the period 1924–1935 and that British industries which had a high three-firm concentration ratio had lower labour productivity relative to the same industry in the United States in 1935–1937. They also presented a number of case studies which led them to conclude that cartelization, weak competition and barriers to entry had adverse implications for productivity outcomes. It is also clear that government-sponsored restraint of competition in coal (Supple, 1987), cotton (Bamberg, 1988) and steel (Tolliday, 1987) was ineffective in promoting productivity improvement through rationalization although this was supposedly a key policy objective. The abandonment of free trade was definitely not an 'infant-industry' policy; in fact, the largest increases in effective protection went to 'old' industries such as hosiery and lace and railway rolling stock (Kitson et al., 1991). A difference-in-differences analysis based on timing and extent of protection of manufactures finds no evidence that tariffs improved productivity performance (Crafts, 2012).

4.4   LONG-TERM IMPLICATIONS OF THE 1930S

The 'managed-economy' strategy for raising the price level in the 1930s was not only understandable as a politically attractive 'short-term fix' but it can also be justified as an appropriate policy stance when nominal interest rates are at the lower bound, and monetary stimulus can only be delivered by lowering real interest rates through increasing inflationary expectations. Eggertsson (2012) provides a model which shows that in such circumstances temporarily allowing firms to exploit market power is welfare improving. His paper notes that once the crisis has passed and the economy has escaped from the liquidity trap normal competition policies should be resumed immediately.

This is, of course, much easier said than done and the British retreat from competition in the 1930s took a very long time to reverse. Average tariff rates on manufacturing imports in the early 1960s were still at mid-1930s levels (Kitson and Solomou, 1990; Morgan and Martin, 1975) while cartelization was also still at mid-1930s levels in the late 1950s.[5] In the early post-war years, there was no appetite for introducing an effective competition policy (Mercer, 1995) and, in general, competition policy remained weak and ineffective until the 1990s, while lack of faith in the market economy saw about 10 per cent of GDP taken into public ownership, which typically entailed a state monopoly.

The political imperative that came from the horrendous experience of unemployment in the 1930s was that, in future, full employment would be the key policy objective. In the famous 1944 White Paper the government made a commitment to 'the maintenance of a high and stable level of employment' (BPP, 1944). Also, it came to be widely believed that Keynesian economics provided policymakers with the tools to achieve this goal.[6] Accordingly, post-war governments thought that failure to do so would mean electoral defeat. The influential analysis of opinion poll data by Goodhart and Bhansali (1970) gives substance to this belief. They found that unemployment greater than 400,000 (about 1.8 per cent of the labour force) implied that the governing party had no chance of leading in the polls; clearly, presiding over a return to interwar levels of unemployment

---

[5]   On the basis of agreements registered under the 1956 legislation, Broadberry and Crafts (2001) estimated that 33.8 per cent of manufacturing was definitely cartelized in the late 1950s and only 27.4 per cent was completely free of any attempt at cartelization.

[6]   Even so, already in the late 1930s and early 1940s, Keynesian economists (notably James Meade) worried about the inflationary consequences of using demand management to reduce unemployment to very low levels, since this would imply wage-push inflation. Some kind of 'wages policy' would be required to deal with this issue (Jones, 1987). In other words, these economists were aware that Keynesian policies would probably entail trying to achieve unemployment rates below the NAIRU.

(never less than 1.8 million) would be electoral suicide. The expansionary fiscal-policy response to quite small increases in unemployment suggests that politicians were well aware of this political arithmetic (Mosley, 1984). During the 1950s and the first half of the 1960s the unemployment rate averaged under 1.6 per cent and was above 2 per cent in only three years.

The 1930s did not see major changes in corporate governance or industrial relations which remained on the long-term trajectories consistent with a 'liberal market economy' established in the nineteenth century. The structure of share ownership moved a bit further in the direction of separation of ownership from control under the impetus of the merger boom of the 1920s, and of heavier taxation which tended to dilute insider holdings somewhat (Cheffins, 2008).[7] A study of large manufacturing and commercial companies in 1936 found that in 48 out of 82 there was a 'dominant ownership interest', that on average the largest shareholder owned 10.3 per cent of the company and that only in seven did the largest 20 shareholders own less than 10 per cent of the shares (Florence, 1961) while the vast majority of shareholders were private individuals rather than institutions. Nevertheless, institutional investors were starting to see the attractions of equities (Scott, 2002), universal suffrage carried the strong possibility of much more progressive taxation and, following the 1931 Royal Mail scandal, accurate disclosure of corporate accounts which would provide the basis for greatly increased merger and acquisition activity was on the horizon (Chambers, 2014). The likelihood of more far-reaching changes in corporate governance had increased significantly.

It might be thought that persistent high unemployment of the interwar period and the unions' defeat in the General Strike of 1926 provided an environment in which the British system of industrial relations would change radically. This was not the case, however; neither the employers nor government attempted significant reform

---

[7] According to the estimates in Hannah (1983), 3,298 firms with a total value of about £550 million disappeared through merger in the 1920s and 1930s.

so the key aspects remained unaltered. The 1927 Trade Disputes and Trade Unions Act left intact the main features of the 1906 Act (Lowe, 1987). Employers sought to assert managerial prerogatives on the shop floor but not to make large investments in new systems of production and managerial control (McKinlay and Zeitlin, 1989). Effort bargains were still made under the auspices of craft unionism but with workers' bargaining power impaired in the years when the labour market was depressed (Lewchuk, 1987).

While the conduct of industrial relations was sensitive to labour market conditions, the structure was still shaped by the inheritance from the nineteenth century. More unskilled workers were unionized and trade union density in the private sector had risen to 30 per cent by 1935 when collective bargaining covered 36 per cent of workers. Nevertheless, in the late 1930s, the modal form of bargaining was multi-unionism and more than 1,000 unions still survived (Gospel, 2005). The government maintained an approach of 'voluntarism' in which industrial relations problems were to be resolved by bargaining between employers and unions with minimal regulation.

At the end of the interwar period, the United Kingdom still had a system of industrial relations characterized by weak managerial control of effort and multi-unionism, while the corporate governance of large companies continued to exhibit a considerable degree of separation of ownership and control. In future, however, these institutional legacies would operate in conditions of generally weak competition in product markets – a situation very different from that prevailing before the First World War. The implication would be more rents to be shared between firms and their workers depending on bargaining power, and more scope for principal–agent problems and managerial failure to proliferate in British industry. Neither of these characteristics could be expected to bode well for productivity performance.

As it turned out, the 'Golden Age' of European growth was just around the corner. In the 1950s and 1960s, Western Europe generally enjoyed unprecedented growth in an episode of rapid catch-up of the

United States. This was, however, a time when the United Kingdom grew relatively slowly and, indeed, experienced its most acute period of relative economic decline. Perhaps this was when the penalties of the early start, working through the interaction of its institutional legacies with weak competition, would really be felt; the more so since the decades after the Second World War were a period when an under-performing liberal market economy confronted a halcyon era for the European coordinated market economies.

4.5 CONCLUSIONS

Growth performance during the interwar years was far from impressive, although in the aggregate there was a small improvement on the disappointing Edwardian period and TFP growth in some sectors, notably in manufacturing, was much improved on the late nineteenth century. The strong recovery from the severe recession of the early 1930s was based on stimulus to aggregate demand from cheap money and then rearmament, rather than faster trend growth of productive potential. Comparisons of productivity performance with the United States show that the United Kingdom failed to match American growth rates. While labour productivity growth in the British economy had risen from 0.5 per cent per year in 1899–1913 to 0.7 per cent per year between 1924 and 1937, the United States achieved 2.4 per cent in the 1920s and 2.5 per cent in the 1930s. Crude TFP growth in British manufacturing at 1.9 per cent per year between 1924 and 1937 was half the American rate of 3.8 per cent per year between 1919 and 1941.

The structure of manufacturing did see an increase in the weight of new industries at the expense of the old staples. Between the Censuses of Production of 1924 and 1935, these new industries experienced considerably faster labour productivity growth, 3.1 per cent per year compared with 1.3 per cent per year and their share of productivity growth in manufacturing amounted to 33.9 per cent.[8] But

---

[8]   Based on an average of 1924 and 1935 weights, see Table 4.6.

overall the impact of this structural change on growth performance was quite modest. Moreover, productivity levels in sectors such as electrical engineering and motor vehicles were further behind those in the United States than was the case for the manufacturing sector as a whole. To suggest that United Kingdom productivity performance in the interwar period was transformed by the contribution of new industries is unrealistic.

Supply-side policy became somewhat more interventionist, especially in the 1930s; although the scale of government intervention was still quite limited compared with the years after the Second World War, it was significantly greater than before 1914. There was more scope, therefore, for errors of commission as well as of omission. It is difficult to see the new stance as positive for medium-term growth outcomes. Industrial policy was defensive and protected declining industries without forcing the exit of the inefficient. The overall implication of the move to a 'managed economy' was a major retreat from competition in product markets which took several decades fully to reverse, and which would prove a serious impediment to productivity performance.

To Richardson (1965) and the 'over-commitment school', the rebalancing of the manufacturing sector towards new industries in the interwar period seemed at last to have ended the unfortunate legacy of the early start. If, however, the problems of the early start were transmitted through institutional channels and constraints on policy, these were intensified rather than eliminated. The opportunity to reform industrial relations while unions were relatively weak was not taken up, the likelihood of a damaging separation of ownership and control in the corporate governance of large companies had increased, and the new political imperative of never again repeating the unemployment experience of outer Britain was about to prove a significant handicap in the design of supply-side policies.

5   Falling Behind in the 'Golden Age'

The period 1950–1973 is conventionally known as the 'golden age' of European economic growth. This was a halcyon period of rapid catch-up growth during which western European economies rapidly reduced the large productivity gap which the United States had established by 1950. Abramovitz and David (1996) suggested European catch-up was based on enhanced 'social capability' and improved 'technological congruence' compared with the interwar period. This meant there was a much greater opportunity for catch-up and European countries were better able to take advantage. During this era of strong β-convergence, which came to an end with the first oil crisis, both real per person and real GDP per hour worked (labour productivity) grew much faster in most European countries than in the United States.

During these years the United Kingdom experienced its fastest ever economic growth but at the same time relative economic decline materialized at a rapid rate vis-à-vis its European peer group such that, by the end of the period it had been overtaken by seven other countries in terms of real GDP per person, and by nine others in terms of labour productivity. The United Kingdom experienced relatively slow growth which is only partly explained by its relatively high income level in 1950. A prima facie case for British 'growth failure' is provided by France and West Germany not just catching up, but overtaking the United Kingdom by 1973 (Table 5.1).

The United Kingdom economic environment continued to be characterized by the retreat from globalization and competition which had developed during the interwar period but economic policy became more ambitious and interventionist as the centre of the political spectrum shifted to the left. This was the era of Beveridge and Keynes in a period which was notable for reduced income inequality

Table 5.1 *Real GDP/person ($GK1990)*

	France	West Germany	UK	USA
1950	5186	4281	6939	9561
1973	12824	13152	12025	16689

Source: Maddison (2010).

and low unemployment. In the early 1960s, in the context of growing concern about comparative economic performance, governments began to experiment with a variety of policies to improve growth outcomes, but in the event, this stopped short of a serious attempt to reform the institutional legacy. Accordingly, the historiography of this period focuses on errors of commission by policymakers.

Several questions arise from this discussion which this chapter will try to answer. How big was the United Kingdom's growth failure during the Golden Age? What were the most important policy mistakes? Did the early start play an important role in exacerbating relative economic decline in these years?

5.1 GROWTH PERFORMANCE IN A EUROPEAN CONTEXT

The Golden Age was a period of macroeconomic stability, notable for the relative absence of financial crises, which followed the traumas of two world wars and the Great Depression. Some have seen this as an episode of fast growth based on a reversion to the pre-1914 trend line (Janossy, 1969) but econometric analysis shows that it was clearly more than this (Mills and Crafts, 2000). That said, countries with relatively large scope for post-war reconstruction such as West Germany, found that this stimulated their growth in the 1950s (Temin, 2002). TFP growth was very rapid during the Golden Age especially in countries with low initial productivity levels. This was based to a large extent on reductions in inefficiency (Jerzmanowski, 2007), especially based on the structural change associated with the shift of labour out of agriculture (Crafts and

Toniolo, 2008). At the same time, technology transfer speeded up as American technology became more cost effective in European conditions, and obstacles to technology transfer were reduced (Nelson and Wright, 1992). European growth was accelerated in these years by trade liberalization which acted to raise the long-run income level.[1] The total long-term effect of reductions in trade protection, including reduction of external tariffs, raised European income levels by nearly 20 per cent by the mid-1970s according to estimates by Badinger (2005). Membership of the European Economic Community (EEC) may have raised income levels of the original six countries by as much as 8 per cent by 1970 (Eichengreen and Boltho, 2008).

In terms of Figure 1.1, European countries had seen substantial shifts in both the Schumpeter and Solow lines and were now characterized by significantly higher λ and s. This is reflected in the shares of investment and R & D expenditure in GDP recorded in Table 5.2. R & D expenditure in the United Kingdom was relatively high and, notably, business-financed R & D was still a larger share of GDP than in France or West Germany in 1967. The weak point was the contribution that this made to productivity growth which was negligible compared with those countries.[2]

Years of schooling were now much higher, albeit slightly lower in 1970 in the United Kingdom than in its peer group (Table 5.2). A crude indicator of the quality of schooling can be obtained from standardized international test scores in mathematics and science, where in the mid-1960s the United Kingdom was a little below France and Germany, but ahead of the United States (Woessmann, 2016). Empirical evidence predicts that the shortfall compared with West Germany would have had a small adverse impact on growth (Hanushek and Woessmann, 2012).[3]

[1]   Trade liberalization had only a transitory effect on growth and did not raise the long-run trend growth rate, cf. Badinger (2005).
[2]   Business R & D was 1.5 per cent of GDP in 1967 compared with 1.1 per cent in both France and West Germany. Verspagen (1996) found the impact of R & D on output growth was not statistically significant in the United Kingdom and the estimated elasticity was tiny, in sharp contrast with the other countries.
[3]   Converted into modern Programme for International Student Assessment (PISA) equivalents, the United Kingdom was in the low 490s while France and West

Table 5.2 *Investment in broad capital, 1970*

	France	West Germany	UK	USA
Non-residential investment (%GDP)	16.3	19.6	14.6	13.5
Years of schooling, ages 15–64	10.4	11.1	10.3	11.1
Higher level qualifications (% workers)	5.6	4.2	8.3	18.7
Intermediate level qualifications (% workers)	54.9	61.2	28.2	17.4
R & D expenditure (%GDP)	1.9	2.1	2.2	2.6

Note: Investment is average of 1960–1973, qualifications data are for 1979.
Sources: Investment from Maddison (1992), schooling from Morrison and Murtin (2009), qualifications from Broadberry and O'Mahony (2007) and R & D from OECD (1991)

Labour force qualifications increased markedly after the Second World War. In 1950, 15.1 per cent of the German labour force had intermediate level or above, whereas at the end of the 1970s this figure had risen to 65.4 per cent. The United Kingdom improved rather less rapidly – the comparable figures were 11.7 per cent in 1950 and 28.6 per cent in the late 1970s. As is reported in Table 5.3, the implication is that in 1973 lower labour quality was an important reason for lower labour productivity in the United Kingdom than in West Germany, although this had not been the case in either 1910 or 1950.

In Table 5.4 we see that, on a growth accounting basis, both France and West Germany achieved contributions to labour productivity growth from both capital deepening and TFP growth which were way ahead of those in the United Kingdom and USA prior to the Second World War (cf. Tables 3.3 and 4.2). The United Kingdom also saw a major increase in these sources of growth to new highs by its

Germany were around 500 (Woessmann, 2016). The regression estimates in Hanushek and Woessmann (2012) indicate that the United Kingdom would suffer a growth penalty of about 0.1 per cent per year.

Table 5.3 *Contributions to labour productivity gap (percentage points)*

	Labour quality	Capital intensity	TFP	Total
USA/UK				
1910	-1.9	30.1	-10.5	17.7
1950	0.3	20.9	45.7	66.9
1973	1.9	10.8	39.6	52.3
Germany/UK				
1910	-0.1	0.2	-24.6	-24.5
1950	-0.6	-2.6	-22.6	-25.6
1973	9.5	5.4	-0.9	14.0

Note: Contributions are derived using a standard growth accounting formula.
Source: Broadberry and O'Mahony (2007).

Table 5.4 *Contributions to labour productivity growth, 1950–1973 (% per year)*

	Education	Capital per hour worked	TFP	Labour productivity growth
France	0.4	1.7	3.1	5.2
West Germany	0.4	2.5	2.5	5.4
UK	0.5	1.5	1.4	3.4
USA	0.3	0.9	1.5	2.7

Note: Estimates are for the market sector.
Sources: O'Mahony (1999) and education contributions derived from Morrisson and Murtin (2009).

own standards, but not to the same extent as leading continental European economies. Relatively slow productivity growth compared with France and West Germany was pervasive across the economy as can be seen in Table 5.5.

During these years Britain experienced its fastest ever economic growth but at the same time relative economic decline proceeded at

Table 5.5 *Crude TFP growth in major sectors, 1950–1973 (% per year)*

	France	West Germany	UK	USA
Agriculture	3.49	3.96	2.53	0.82
Mining	–0.36	2.28	0.46	0.97
Manufacturing	4.22	4.12	3.28	1.95
Construction	2.67	1.86	1.03	0.52
Utilities	7.17	3.33	3.36	3.45
Transport and communications	4.40	3.92	2.31	2.26
Distributive trades	1.75	1.79	0.78	1.02
Market sector	3.49	2.92	1.87	1.77
GDP	3.10	3.76	1.74	1.49

Source: O'Mahony (1999).

a rapid rate vis-à-vis its European peer group such that, by the end of the period Britain had been overtaken by seven other countries in terms of real GDP per person and by nine others in terms of labour productivity. United Kingdom growth was slower by at least 0.7 percentage points per year compared with any other country, including those who started the period with similar or higher income levels. The proximate reasons for relatively slow labour productivity growth were weak capital per worker and TFP growth compared with more successful economies like West Germany. Maddison (1996) attempted a decomposition of the sources of TFP growth and he concluded that the shortfall in Britain could not be explained away by lower scope for catch-up or the structure of the economy, although clearly rapid TFP growth in countries like West Germany did reflect reconstruction, reductions in the inefficient allocation of resources and lower initial productivity (Temin, 2002).

Although slower growth can be partly explained by virtue of a higher initial level of income and productivity, being overtaken by France and West Germany is a clear indicator of avoidable failure. This is confirmed by an unconditional growth regression reported by Crafts and Toniolo (2008) for a cross-section of regions within European countries in 1950–1973, where growth of real GDP per person is related to the level of GDP in 1950 as a percentage of that in the United States and country dummy variables:

$$GYP = 5.29 - 0.03\ Y/P + 0.92\ \text{Spain} + 1.045\ \text{West Germany} - 0.83\ \text{UK}$$
$$(17.6)\ (-7.5)\qquad (3.5)\qquad\quad (4.3)\qquad\qquad\qquad\quad (-3.5)$$
$$+\ 0.72\ \text{Italy} + 0.17\ \text{France}\qquad R^2 = 0.870,\ N = 85$$
$$(3.0)\qquad\quad (0.77)$$

where the omitted-country dummy variable is Netherlands. This suggests that there was a growth failure of about 0.8 percentage points per year in the United Kingdom cumulating to an income shortfall of almost 20 per cent by 1973.[4]

5.2 THE EICHENGREEN HYPOTHESIS

The most striking hypothesis to explain enhanced social capability in post-war Western Europe is that of Eichengreen (1996) who argued that high investment rates which allowed successful exploitation of catch-up opportunities were facilitated by successful social contracts which sustained wage moderation by workers in return for high investment by firms. These 'corporatist' arrangements provided institutions to monitor capitalists' compliance and centralized wage bargaining which protected high investment firms and prevented free-riding by subsets of workers. In addition, the state provided 'bonds' that would be jeopardized if labour defected on the agreements in the form of an expanded welfare state. The central foundation of a cooperative equilibrium with high investment and wage moderation is that both sides are patient and take a long-term view of the payoffs to their decisions (cf. Appendix 1) and the implication in terms of Figure 1.1 is a significant upward shift of the Solow line.

---

[4]   This is large enough to be a real cause for concern but it is also fair to say that 'decline' is an ideological construct which has been associated with the politicization of economic policy (Tomlinson, 1996).

It is certainly true that corporatist industrial relations were quite widespread in the Golden Age; Crouch (1993) puts Austria, Belgium, Netherlands, Switzerland, West Germany and the Scandinavian economies in this category. In a growth-regression study, Gilmore (2009) found that coordinated wage bargaining may have had positive effects on investment and growth prior to 1975 but not subsequently.[5] The wage moderation/high investment equilibrium was fragile and it did not generally survive the turbulence of the 1970s, a time when union militancy and union power rose dramatically, as did labour's share of value added, and the rewards for patience fell in conditions of greater capital mobility, floating exchange rates and greater employment protection. At the same time, the corporatist model of economic growth was becoming less appropriate by the 1970s in economies which had markedly reduced the productivity gap with the United States and now needed to become more innovative and less reliant on technology transfer, as Eichengreen (2007) himself pointed out.

The key point is that coordinated market economies (CMEs) were well positioned for rapid catch-up growth during the Golden Age and more likely to sustain a cooperative equilibrium between capital and labour. Hall and Soskice (2001) describe the archetypal CME as having a set of complementary institutions that deliver patient capital and wage moderation together with high levels of investment in specific human capital in firms and incremental innovation. The basis for this is bank finance with block holdings of shares, corporatist industrial relations, strong coordination of employers and cooperative inter-firm relations. This can be described as a system of 'inside control'. By contrast, the complementary institutions of the archetypal liberal market economy (LME) feature equity finance with diffuse shareholdings, general human capital formation in colleges, strong competition between firms and deregulated, flexible labour markets. This is

---

[5] However, this was not the only route to rapid catch-up growth. In other countries, for example, Italy, growth was promoted by industrialization based on elastic supplies of labour and undervalued currencies which underpinned investment and TFP growth and also restrained wage increases at least until the late 1960s (Crafts and Magnani, 2013).

a system of 'outside control' with much greater asymmetry of information between managers and owners, with a tendency to prefer early payoffs to investment. The advantages of these arrangements are in radical innovation and rapid adjustment to new circumstances.

Golden-Age Germany epitomizes the relative strengths of a CME. Compared with the United Kingdom, it invested more both in physical capital and labour force training (cf. Table 5.2). By 1973, it had opened up a labour productivity gap with the United Kingdom based on labour force skills and capital. By contrast, it did not have an advantage over the United Kingdom in the level of TFP. As a leading LME, the United States outperformed the United Kingdom in terms of technology (and TFP) and its labour-quality advantage was based on a much higher proportion of college-educated workers.

The institutional legacy bequeathed to post-war Britain was obviously much closer to the LME than the CME stereotype, as the discussion in Chapter 4 underlined. This was not an economy with a high degree of patience either among investors or workers. In a situation where it is not possible to write binding contracts, either the absence of unions or strong corporatist trade unionism would have been preferable to the idiosyncratic British industrial relations system. This can easily be understood in terms of the Eichengreen model or an extension of it to incorporate endogenous innovation. In the United Kingdom, it was generally not possible to make the cooperative deals to underpin investment and innovation because bargaining took place with multiple unions or with shop stewards representing subsets of a firm's work force who could not internalize the benefits of wage restraint. This exposed sunk-cost investments to a 'hold-up' problem.[6]

---

[6] In the endogenous innovation framework the 'hold-up' arises when after a successful innovation workers use their bargaining power to extract a share of the profits. This reduces the incentive to innovate and thus the rate of growth. The more unions are involved in the bargaining, the more profits are reduced. The problem can be eliminated if a binding contract prevents renegotiation or there is no union or if a cooperative equilibrium is achieved with a single union. For a formal model and empirical evidence, see Bean and Crafts (1996).

If this was the moment when, as the Eichengreen hypothesis implies, the CME came into its own, then this was also the point at which the penalty of the early start came through. At the same time, the United Kingdom was lacking a key ingredient of a successful LME, namely, strong competition in product markets.

5.3 SUPPLY-SIDE POLICY PROBLEMS

Critics of the pre-1914 British economy typically complain about market failure and lack of effective government action to correct it. In the post-1945 context of a mixed economy with an enhanced role for government intervention, the problems increasingly seemed to be of government failure. 'Government failure' occurs where the choice or implementation of policy leads to outcomes that are inefficient.[7] The standard reasons for government failure include inadequate information, inexperience, principal-agent problems (inability to incentivize officials to work effectively), asymmetric lobbying, inability to make credible commitments, and vote-seeking by politicians. Areas of concern include the structure of taxation, the performance of nationalized industries, industrial policy, competition policy and international trade policy.

The context for post-war taxation was a much increased level of public expenditure. Through to the mid-1960s public expenditure was around 38 per cent of GDP compared with a pre-war figure of 26 per cent (social = 10.5 per cent of GDP) and then rose to 43 per cent (social = 21.5 per cent of GDP) in 1973. The increase was matched by a similar rise in the tax take which came chiefly from taxes on income. Broadly speaking, the rise in public expenditure was associated with the expansion of the welfare state which was funded by increases in direct taxation. In other words, there was much more redistribution of income. All this was not really surprising in the context of the change in the median voter and shift in the centre of the political spectrum since Edwardian times. Although these

---

[7] For a textbook treatment see Wallis and Dollery (1999).

changes were instigated by Labour, they were accepted by the Conservatives and they were not vastly out of line with other European countries.

A tax system more conducive to growth would have broadened the tax base, reduced high marginal tax rates, and shifted the balance away from direct to indirect taxation. In this regard, Tanzi (1969) was highly critical of income tax on the grounds that it featured very high marginal rates – the top rate was 97.5 per cent in 1949 and 88.75 per cent in 1973 – he described the system as the least growth friendly of all the countries included in his study. Another notable failure was the long delay before Value Added Tax was finally introduced in 1973. Nominal rates of corporate income taxation were also high – at least 40 per cent in each year and as high as 56.25 per cent at the peak. However, especially in the 1960s and 1970s, effective marginal corporate tax rates were much lower in the light of generous depreciation allowances and high inflation – on average as low as 3.7 per cent by 1980 (King and Fullerton, 1984). The issue here was that large distortions arose through the varying treatment given to different types of investment. Much of this diagnosis was shared by the politicians of the day, especially in the Conservative Party, but such changes were felt to be vote losers and, in particular, to be unwelcome to trade union leaders (Daunton, 2002).

A flagship policy of the Attlee government was the nationalization of a substantial component of the United Kingdom economy including public utilities and transport during the late 1940s. This meant that a sizeable fraction of investment would be undertaken by the state rather than the private sector. In a typical post-war year (1971), the nationalized industries accounted for 18.7 per cent of investment, 7.2 per cent of employment and 10.2 per cent of GDP (Corti, 1976). With the exception of the coal industry, the nationalization of which was a concession to a powerful trade union, there was a market-failure rationale (natural monopoly, externalities) for the enterprises taken into state ownership (Millward, 1997) and, in ignorance of the serious principal-agent problems which would proliferate under state ownership, such actions were favoured by many economists at the time (Shleifer, 1998).

By the 1970s, it was clear that this was an experiment that had failed. The productivity and financial performance of nationalized industries was deeply disappointing. Both inefficient use of labour and excessive investment were serious problems (Vickers and Yarrow, 1988). In 1973 TFP in electricity, gas and water (UK = 100) was 219 in the United States, 119 in West Germany and 88 in France. The figures for labour productivity were 370, 134 and 143, respectively. In every case these productivity gaps far exceed those in manufacturing (O'Mahony, 1999). It became apparent that pricing and investment rules were flouted either by management or through political interference (NEDO, 1976). This amounted to ownership without effective control. The Conservatives did not seriously contemplate privatization, a policy which would have been anathema to the trade union movement.

Over time in the context of pursuing policies which were acceptable to both sides of industry, there was an increasing emphasis on the use of 'industrial policy' to promote faster growth. 'Industrial policy' aims to change the distribution of resources across economic sectors and activities (Warwick, 2013). Thus, it includes both 'horizontal' policies which focus on activities such as innovation, investment and education, while 'selective' policies aim to increase the size of particular sectors. Selective policies may try to help struggling sectors faced with downsizing or may seek to develop new competitive advantages. The classic justification for industrial policy is that it remedies market failures, for example, by providing public goods, solving coordination problems or subsidizing activities with positive externalities. More generally, the development of endogenous-growth theory suggests that horizontal policies which raise the appropriable rate of return to innovation and/or investment can have positive effects on the rate of growth. On the other hand, as British experience underlines, there is a high risk of government failure as decisions are distorted by rent-and vote-seeking.

Throughout the period, policies were adopted to enhance investment-led growth with a variety of subsidies to investment in the form of depreciation allowances or grants. At their peak in 1978 these subsidies amounted to 10 per cent of fixed investment but they are widely thought to have been a badly designed policy which was poorly targeted. The econometric evidence is that they had little effect on the volume of investment over the long run (Sumner, 1999) with the implication that there was a large deadweight cost.

In addition, selective policies were used increasingly over time but also with little success. Although 'picking winners' may have been the aspiration, "it was losers like Rolls Royce, British Leyland and Alfred Herbert who picked Ministers" (Morris and Stout, 1985, p. 873). There was a very clear tendency for selective subsidies to be skewed towards relatively few industries, notably aircraft, shipbuilding and, latterly, motor vehicles (Wren, 1996a). More generally, there was quite a strong bias towards shoring up ailing industries which is well reflected in the portfolio of holdings of the National Enterprise Board (Wren, 1996b), in the pattern of tariff protection across sectors (Greenaway and Milner, 1994), and in the nationalization of British Leyland.[8] Moreover, policies to subsidize British high-technology industries were notably unsuccessful in this period in a number of cases including civil aircraft, which by 1974 had cost £1.5 billion at 1974 prices for a return of £0.14 billion (Gardner, 1976), computers (Hendry, 1989) and nuclear power (Cowan, 1990).[9] A horizontal policy such as an R & D tax credit would surely have been more appropriate than vain attempts to create 'national champions'.

A key feature of the Golden-Age British economy was the weakness of competition in product markets which had developed in the 1930s and intensified subsequently. Competition policy was largely ineffective and market power was substantial. Competition policy

[8]   It is in fact quite predictable that declining industries will take the lion's share of support from selective industrial policies (Baldwin and Robert-Nicoud, 2007) but this was not perhaps obvious before these policies were tried and failed.

[9]   Concorde and the Advanced Gas-Cooled Reactor were egregious policy errors (Henderson, 1977).

was inaugurated with the Monopolies and Restrictive Practices Commission in 1948, evolved through the Restrictive Practices Act (1956) and the Monopolies and Mergers Commission (1965), but was mostly ineffective (Clarke et al., 1998). Few investigations took place, very few mergers were prevented, the process was politicized, a variety of 'public-interest' defences for anti-competitive activities were allowed, and there were no penalties for bad behaviour. Only the Restrictive Practices Act had teeth but its attack on collusion was ultimately undermined by cartels being superseded by mergers. Competition policy was not seen by economists at this time as important for productivity performance (Broadberry and Crafts, 2001) while neither big business nor the trade union movement had any great enthusiasm for aggressive measures which might threaten their supernormal profits and wages (Mercer, 1995).

Not surprisingly, there is evidence that the British economy was characterized by substantial market power in this period. Initially, collusive activity was widespread; an examination of the agreements registered in compliance with the 1956 Act shows that only 27 per cent of manufacturing was free of price-fixing and 35.7 per cent was cartelized (Broadberry and Crafts, 2001). Over time, industrial concentration increased steadily such that the average 3-firm concentration ratio across manufacturing sectors was 41 per cent by 1968 compared with 26 per cent in 1935 (Clarke, 1985). Crafts and Mills (2005) estimated that the price-cost margin in United Kingdom manufacturing during 1954–1973 averaged over 2 compared with around 1.1 in West Germany which is consistent with the finding in Geroski and Jacquemin (1988) that the magnitude and persistence of supernormal profits for large firms during 1949 to 1977 was large in the United Kingdom but that significant deviations from competitive outcomes were not observed in West Germany in the 1960s and 1970s.[10]

[10]   The existence of significant market power in the UK but not in West Germany at this time is confirmed by the similarity of the primal and dual measures of TFP in the latter but not in the former; see Crafts and Mills (2005) for further elaboration.

The evidence is that weak competition had an adverse effect on United Kingdom productivity performance during the Golden Age. Broadberry and Crafts (1996) found that cartelization was strongly negatively related to productivity growth in a cross section of manufacturing industries for 1954–63. This result is borne out by the difference-in-differences analysis in Symeonidis (2008) who showed that when cartels were abandoned following the 1956 Restrictive Practices Act labour productivity growth in formerly-colluding sectors rose by 1.8 percentage points per year in 1964–1973 compared with 1954–1963. This finding suggests that a more vigorous competition policy would have improved productivity performance.

Weak competition in product markets was buttressed by protectionism which the United Kingdom was very slow to give up by comparison with its European peer group. Delayed entry to the EEC which the United Kingdom did not join until 1973 was an important part of this. Accordingly, average tariff rates on United Kingdom manufactures were still 14.5 per cent in 1960 compared with 14.7 per cent in 1935 and a comparison for 1958 showed tariffs were typically 2 to 3 times the rate for the same industrial sector in West Germany. Whereas trade costs fell dramatically within the EEC in the 1960s for the United Kingdom this was delayed until the 1970s (Crafts, 2012, Table 2.5). Failure to liberalize trade underpinned market power as reflected by high price-cost margins (Hitiris, 1978).

Ex-post analysis suggests that joining the EEC raised the level of United Kingdom GDP by about 8 to 10 per cent notably through increasing the volume of trade and strengthening competition (Crafts, 2016). Realizing this gain earlier would have made relative economic decline during the Golden Age a good deal less acute. However, this outcome is much better than was predicted by economists ex ante; in the early 1970s, the economic case for EEC entry appeared finely balanced. By then, however, there was considerable business support in view of anticipated profits from better market access (Rollings, 2007).

As this discussion has revealed, there were numerous reasons for government failure during the 'Golden Age'. Nevertheless, there was also a common factor which informed these policies, namely, a desire to not to upset organized labour and, indeed, even a willingness to accept an implicit trade union veto on policy reforms. This makes sense given the electoral importance that was attached to short-run macroeconomic outcomes, especially the imperative of achieving a very low rate of unemployment without igniting inflation. This encouraged successive governments, notably in the 1950s and the 1970s, to seek wage restraint through accepting serious constraints on economic policy (Flanagan et al., 1983).[11] The policy worked initially in the sense that the 'post-war settlement' reduced the Non-accelerating Inflation Rate of Unemployment (NAIRU) quite considerably and permitted the very low levels of unemployment seen in the 1950s (Broadberry, 1994) but in the long run there was a significant cost in terms of inferior productivity performance.

5.4 CORPORATE GOVERNANCE, INDUSTRIAL RELATIONS AND COMPETITION

During the Golden Age the United Kingdom can be described as a malfunctioning LME. The inheritance from the nineteenth century remained in terms of the basic structure of financial markets and trade unionism but some aspects of both corporate governance and industrial relations became less conducive to good productivity performance. A major change from the early twentieth century was that these institutions were now situated in an environment of much weaker competition in product markets.

In these post-war decades, the main developments in terms of corporate governance were a much more pronounced separation of ownership from control in large companies, a ferocious merger boom and the advent of the hostile takeover. Fewer large companies were

---

[11] A classic example is the abandonment in 1952 by the new Conservative government of the ROBOT scheme to float the pound which was seen by its supporters as integral to strengthening the role of market forces in the economy (Bulpitt and Burnham, 1999).

owner-controlled than the 58.5 per cent of Florence's 1936 sample. In 1951 he found this share had fallen to 40.8 per cent (Florence, 1961) and subsequent studies on a similar basis for the late 1960s (Radice, 1971) and mid-1970s (Nyman and Silberston, 1978) reported 32.6 and 38.5 per cent, respectively.[12] This reflected the retreat of family ownership, the dilution of equity holdings through mergers, a tax system which now hugely favoured institutional rather than individual share ownership and an environment of financial repression and inflation which led to financial institutions re-balancing their portfolios towards equities (Cheffins, 2008). In 1957 individuals and financial institutions held 65.8 and 21.6 per cent of shares, respectively, whereas by 1975 these fractions were 37.5 and 48.0 per cent, respectively (Chambers, 2014). Outside control became prevalent in quoted companies and the separation of ownership and control intensified especially because financial institutions were notoriously passive investors.

Firm disappearances by merger reached record levels during the 1960s and early 1970s. During 1960–1973, on average, 549 firms with a share value at 1961 prices of £531.6 million disappeared through merger each year (Hannah, 1983). The existence of an effective market for corporate control is indeed a key aspect of outside control of managers. However, the evidence strongly suggests that this market did not work efficiently to discipline bad managers and remove poor performers. Size rather than efficiency or long-term investment was the key to survival (Singh, 1975). Mergers did not generally deliver productivity gains (Meeks, 1977) but were the result of management pursuing its own interests rather than those of the shareholders (Newbould, 1970).

These decades represent the apogee of strong but decentralized collective bargaining in the United Kingdom (Crouch, 1993). The modal form was still multi-unionism but more workers belonged

[12]   Nyman and Silberston (1978) actually reported an estimate of 52.6 per cent but they used different criteria. If the data in their paper are analysed on a similar basis to Florence, this falls to 38.5 per cent.

to trade unions (46 per cent of private sector employees by 1972) while the coverage of collective agreements increased (70 per cent in 1972). The big change was the rise of the shop steward with an estimated 175,000 in 1968 and linked to this an explosion of individual plant bargaining including over both pay and work practices. Unions became bigger but, even so, there were still 454 in 1972 (Gospel, 2005). For much of the period governments steered clear of industrial relations reform and respected the hallowed tradition of 'voluntarism'. This was hardly surprising given the prevailing approach of seeking wage moderation in striving for full employment with low inflation. Trade unions continued to enjoy the legal immunities given by the 1906 Trade Disputes Act. In the later 1960s, however, in the face of increased militancy and the inability or unwillingness of trade union leaders to deliver on wage restraint, political pressure to legislate grew and eventually the 1971 Industrial Relations Act was introduced. This act was only a modest attempt at reform but was a failure in the face of union opposition and lack of enthusiasm by employers and was repealed in 1974.

Given that bargaining now took place in an environment characterized by tight labour markets and considerable market power for firms, we might expect high rents of which unions could expect a large share at a time when their bargaining power was strong (Blanchflower et al., 1996). In so far as they used this to bargain for lower work effort (overstaffing) or to resist the introduction of new working practices then weak competition would undermine productivity performance (Machin and Wadhwani, 1989). Where competition is weak the principal-agent problems that arise from weak shareholders and managerial control are exacerbated (Nickell, 1996) and market discipline to prevent slow or inefficient adoption of new technology is undermined (Aghion et al., 1997). Competition also promotes good management practices which payoff in productivity outcomes (Bloom and van Reenen, 2007). Although economic theory is ambivalent about the impact of competition on R & D, entry threats can be expected to promote innovation to protect future rents if firm survival is thought to be feasible (Aghion and Howitt, 2006).

Thus, we might expect productivity performance in the post-war British economy to be adversely affected by the interaction of the institutional legacies in respect of corporate governance and industrial relations together with full employment and weak competition. This would seem to be a recipe for a malfunctioning LME. And indeed the empirical evidence lends considerable support to this diagnosis.

Econometric studies have shown the following. First, greater competition raised productivity growth where firms did not have a dominant external shareholder (Nickell et al., 1997). In this (typical) case, a fall in supernormal profits from 15 to 5 per cent of value added raised TFP growth by 1 per percentage point per year. Moreover, increases in interest payments relative to cash flow also promoted significantly faster productivity growth.[13] Second, greater competition was good for innovation. Geroski (1990) found that, once differences in technological opportunity across industries were taken into account, in the 1970s the positive effects of market power working through expected profits were heavily outweighed by negative effects on managerial effort. Third, Bean and Crafts (1996) examined the consequences of multiple unions for TFP growth in an endogenous-innovation setting where, in the absence of binding contracts, it is predicted that innovative effort will be reduced by the expectation that the workforce will appropriate some of the gains. They found that the presence of multiple unions lowered TFP growth by 0.75 to 1 percentage point per year in the 1954–1979 period.

Case studies strongly implicate bad management and restrictive labour practices resulting from bargaining with unions in poor productivity outcomes. Pratten and Atkinson (1976) reviewed 25 studies of which 23 reported inefficient use of labour, in 21 cases from failings

---

[13]   This suggests that principal-agent problems were an issue when management was in the comfort zone. It also implies that industrial subsidies which eased financial pressures were potentially detrimental to productivity performance consistent with the prediction in Aghion et al. (1997) for the agency-problem case.

of management and in 14 instances from restrictive labour practices. Inefficient use of labour and industrial relations problems accounted for a significant productivity gap in multinational companies between British plants and those in Germany or the United States in 1972 (Pratten, 1976) which would not have surprised the business respondents to an Oxford survey in the late 1940s who thought such problems were prevalent (Andrews and Brunner, 1950). A strong theme in several studies which highlight low effort bargains is that they were sustained by the weakness of competition; for example, this emerges clearly in the study by Zweig (1951) and also in the seminal work in industrial sociology on restrictive labour practices (Lupton, 1963). A notable aspect of these bargains is that potential productivity gains from new technology were impaired (Prais, 1981). In a well-known and egregious case, motor vehicles, management completely lost control of effort norms in the switch to measured day work with disastrous consequences for productivity (Lewchuk, 1987).

In sum, the evidence is that multi-unionism and the separation of ownership and control adversely affected United Kingdom productivity performance during the Golden Age. Corporate governance and industrial relations were clearly recognizable as the grandchildren of their Victorian predecessors but having mutated into more problematic forms and with a greater downside in the environment of weak competition that prevailed in these early post-war decades. In terms of Figure 1.1, this unfortunate combination of institutions and policy significantly reduced λ.

5.5 CONCLUSIONS

The years from 1950 to 1973 saw the fastest ever growth of real GDP per person in the United Kingdom. Even so, it was a period of acute relative economic decline during which rivals like France and West Germany grew much faster and eventually overtook the United Kingdom in terms of income levels. Seen in terms of the scope for catch-up growth, the United Kingdom underperformed to the extent of a shortfall of probably around 0.8 per cent per year with the implication that the level of GDP per person was at least 20 per cent below what would have been reasonable to expect at the end of the Golden Age.

By the 1960s, slow growth was recognized as a problem by British governments but the design of supply-side policy left a lot to be desired throughout the period. Marginal income tax rates were too high, the productivity record of the nationalized industries was undermined by principal-agent problems, investment subsidies were badly targeted, selective industrial policy was politicized and deservedly got a bad name, industrial relations continued to be unreformed, competition policy was too weak and protectionism was reversed much too slowly. In terms of Figure 1.1, this policy configuration implied a downward shift of the Schumpeter line. There were a number of reasons for government failure but an important constraint on policy design resulted from politicians' fear of unemployment and the perceived need to persuade trade unions to exercise wage restraint.

A key feature of this policy configuration is that it implied that competition was impaired across much of the economy. The interaction of weak competition with institutional legacies in the corporate governance of large companies and the system of industrial relations was not favourable for productivity performance. It allowed bad management to persist in an era of weak shareholders and provided supernormal profits which were shared with multiple unions in higher wages and lower effort. This implied that the productivity potential of new technology was less than fully realized. Nor was a cooperative equilibrium (with high investment by firms and wage restraint by workers) feasible. In the policy environment engendered by the inescapable experience of the 1930s and the shifting centre ground of politics, the outcome was a malfunctioning LME. Rather than the early twentieth century, the Golden Age after the Second World War was the point at which the downside of the early start was felt most severely.

APPENDIX I

Cameron and Wallace (2002) provide a game-theoretic version of Eichengreen's argument that a co-operative equilibrium which entailed high investment in return for wage moderation underwrote high investment in Golden-Age Europe.

The idea is to model a situation where it is profitable for a firm to invest if the union selects a low wage claim but not if the union makes an aggressive pay claim. In addition, if the union knows for sure that the firm would invest rather than pay profits out as dividends a lower pay claim would be optimal. The wage moderation/high investment equilibrium is Pareto-dominant. This requires the two conditions

$$(\text{Firm})\, \delta_F \pi(w_0, L_0) > I > \delta_F \pi\Big(w_H, L(w_H)\Big)$$

$$(\text{Union})\, (1 + \delta_U) w_0 L_0 > w_H L_0 + \delta_U w_H L(w_H)$$

where I is the investment, δ_F and δ_U are, respectively, the firm and union discount factors where a higher value implies greater patience, π is the profit function, and w_0, L_0 and w_H, L_H are the wage bills associated with the profit-maximizing employment level chosen by the firm at low and high wages, respectively. The two conditions imply that discounted profits and the discounted sum of total wages are higher with investment and wage moderation.

If, as is likely, the payoffs are subject to some uncertainty, then the equilibrium that is chosen will be based on risk-dominance. This implies that the wage restraint/ high investment equilibrium is chosen if and only if

$$[\delta_F \pi(w_0, L_0) - I][(1 + \delta_U) w_0, L_0 - w_H, L_H - \delta_U w_H, L(w_H)]$$
$$> [I - \delta_F \pi\Big(w_H, L(w_H)\Big)](w_H - w_0) L_0$$

In the case where $f(L) = AL^\alpha$ this condition can be re-stated as

$$\left(\delta_F / \delta_U\right)[(1 + \delta_U) w_0 - w_H] L_0 > |(\alpha/(1 - \alpha))$$

where $L_0 = (\alpha A / w_0)^{1/(1 - \alpha)}$.

This formulation implies that defection from the wage restraint/high investment equilibrium is more likely if δ_F, δ_U, or A decrease or w_H increases. Thus, the good outcome is less likely when firms and/or workers become more impatient, in the case of adverse technology shocks or when unions' bargaining power goes up.

The Eichengreen hypothesis that centralized wage bargaining is conducive to the high investment/wage moderation equilibrium might be interpreted as a prediction that δ_U and δ_F will be high. However, other aspects of the Golden Age economic environment are clearly relevant and these might include restricted capital mobility as positive for δ_U the fixed exchange rate regime as a constraint on w_H, and nice technology surprises as positive for A.

Key implications of this formulation are that the good equilibrium is quite fragile and that formulating a decisive test of the Eichengreen hypothesis is not straightforward. However, this set-up does help to explain why the end of the restricted capital-mobility, fixed-exchange rate Bretton Woods system in the early 1970s may have undermined the co-operative equilibrium.

6   From the Golden Age to the Financial Crisis

After the early 1970s, growth slowed down markedly right across Europe. The end of the Golden Age had a number of unavoidable aspects including the exhaustion of transitory components of fast growth such as post-war reconstruction, reduced opportunities to redeploy labour out of agriculture, narrowing of the technology gap and diminishing returns to investment. Moreover, the United States itself experienced a productivity growth slowdown. All-in-all, the scope for catch-up growth was considerably reduced, although by no means eliminated, and in terms of Figure 1.1, both the Schumpeter and the Solow lines experienced adverse shifts. Contrary to what might have been expected in the 1970s, growth in the United Kingdom suffered less of a decrease in the following 30 years and relative economic decline ceased at least for a while.

Two key surprises shaped this reversal of fortunes, namely, the Thatcher experiment and the ICT revolution. These entailed, respectively, the 'end of the post-war consensus' and a new general purpose technology. Since New Labour largely accepted the reforms of the 1980s, there were not only significant but sustained changes in supply-side policy as well as opportunities for business to transform production, plus some synergies between these developments. In the context of the 'third industrial revolution', there was a distinct possibility that relative economic performance might once again change. Might ICT play more to the strengths of an LME than a CME?

Buoyed by the contribution of ICT, growth of real GDP per person was apparently quite robust from the mid-1990s to the financial crisis. Some even claimed that boom and bust had been abolished, but then it all ended in tears. Since 2007, productivity growth has been in the doldrums and the economy has endured its worst post-war recession. Now, there is a quite widespread belief that the 'new normal' is an era of low growth or even 'secular stagnation'.

This discussion prompts several questions to be addressed in this chapter. Did United Kingdom growth performance actually improve after the Golden Age? How far was Thatcherism an effective antidote to relative economic decline? Do the 2007–2008 crisis and its aftermath reveal that growth prior to this was 'too good to be true'?

6.1 GROWTH PERFORMANCE: THE END OF RELATIVE ECONOMIC DECLINE

After the 1970s, real GDP per person in the United Kingdom was no longer falling relative to its peer group. The income levels reported in Table 6.1 for 2007 show more favourable ratios for the United Kingdom relative to the other three countries than had been the case in 1973.[1] As can be seen in Table 6.2, after the Golden Age each of these countries grew more slowly for the next 20 years or so. United Kingdom growth slowed down less than was the case in France or West Germany so relative performance improved. In the context of the ICT revolution, from the mid-1990s, growth of real GDP per person revived in the United Kingdom and USA but not in France or Germany so this was the point at which income gaps between the United Kingdom and continental Europe were reduced significantly.

Slower growth was accompanied by smaller shares of non-residential investment in GDP, as is reported in Table 6.3. The difference between the United Kingdom and its European peer group was much smaller at the turn of the century than at the end of the Golden Age (cf. Table 5.2). These figures, however, only cover tangible capital

---

[1] These calculations are at purchasing-power-parity-adjusted exchange rates. As is noted in the table, this conversion is done in a different way for the last two rows of the table using 2015$EKS whereas the first two rows are measured in terms of 1990$GK. If this method had also been used for the later years, the United Kingdom comes out better relative to France and Germany and would in fact be ahead of West Germany in 2007. The comparison with the United States is only marginally affected. There is clearly a significant index number problem here which deserves further research. The comparisons presented in the table are chosen to guard against overstatement of the United Kingdom's improved position.

Table 6.1 *Real GDP per person*

	France	Germany	UK	USA
1973	12824	13152	12025	16689
1995 (1)	18318	17127	17599	24712
1995 (2)	32636	36216	30232	41861
2007	40143	43558	40697	54093

Notes: 1973 and 1995 (1) are in 1990$GK. 1995 (2) and 2007 are in 2015$EKS. Estimate is for West Germany in 1973.
Sources: Maddison (2010) and The Conference Board (2016).

Table 6.2 *Rates of growth of real GDP/person and real GDP/hour worked (% per year)*

	Y/P	Y/HW
1950–1973		
France	4.02	5.29
Germany	5.00	5.91
UK	2.42	2.81
USA	2.45	2.57
1973–1995		
France	1.65	2.67
Germany	1.76	2.86
UK	1.76	2.40
USA	1.81	1.27
1995–2007		
France	1.70	1.77
Germany	1.54	1.70
UK	2.41	2.09
USA	2.18	2.30
2007–2016		
France	0.06	0.66
Germany	0.84	0.68
UK	0.19	0.09
USA	0.46	0.85

Note: Germany is West Germany prior to 1995.
Source: The Conference Board (2017).

Table 6.3 *Investment in broad capital, c. 2000*

	France	Germany	UK	USA
Non-residential investment (%GDP)	11.7	12.5	11.6	12.0
Years of schooling, ages 15–64	12.0	13.0	13.1	13.0
PISA score	496	510	505	482
Higher level qualifications (% workers)	11.7	8.2	18.6	27.6
Intermediate level qualifications (% workers)	67.3	71.7	37.0	25.3
Investment in intangibles (% market sector GDP)	7.9	7.2	10.5	11.5
R & D expenditure (%GDP)	2.2	2.5	1.8	2.7

Note: Investment is average of 1999–2003, Programme for International Student Assessment (PISA) scores are the average of mathematics and science in 2006.
Sources: Investment from OECD National Accounts database, schooling from Morrison and Murtin (2009), PISA score from OECD PISA 2006, qualifications from Broadberry and O'Mahony (2007), intangible investment from van Ark et al. (2009), R & D from OECD Main Science and Technology Indicators.

whereas, by the early twenty-first century investment in intangibles in the United Kingdom was nearly as big and was a larger share of GDP than in France or Germany so that the total United Kingdom investment rate exceeded these countries.[2] By contrast, United Kingdom investment in R & D as a share of GDP had fallen compared with 1970 and was lower in 2000 than in France, Germany and the United States and less than half the proportion in the leading country, Sweden. Since R & D investments are estimated to have a very high social rate of return this represents a disappointing United Kingdom weakness (Frontier Economics, 2014).

[2]   Investment in intangible capital comprises computerized information (including software), innovative property (including R & D and design) and economic competencies (including advertising, training and reorganization).

Table 6.4 *Contributions to labour productivity gap (percentage points)*

	Labour quality	Capital intensity	TFP	Total
USA/UK				
1973	1.9	10.8	39.6	52.3
2000	0.4	12.6	11.3	24.3
Germany/UK				
1973	9.5	5.4	−0.9	14.0
2000	3.7	11.7	1.4	16.8

Note: Capital intensity is based on tangible capital only; contributions are derived using a standard growth accounting formula.
Source: Broadberry and O'Mahony (2007).

With regard to human capital, years of schooling of the United Kingdom working-age population had risen by almost three years in 2000 compared with 1970 which was a little bit more than the increases recorded in the other countries listed in Table 6.3. Cognitive skills of schoolchildren as measured by PISA scores were intermediate between France and Germany but well ahead of the United States. Qualifications of the labour force had improved considerably in the United Kingdom as well as its comparators with a continuation of the pattern with the United Kingdom having a larger share of higher level qualifications, boosted by an expansion of college education, but a much lower share of intermediate level qualifications than Germany. Interestingly, in 2000 a shortfall of physical capital contributed more than labour quality to the labour productivity gap of the United Kingdom with Germany (Table 6.4).

After 1973, labour productivity growth slowed down in European countries with declines in the contributions both of capital deepening and also, especially, TFP growth, as is shown in Table 6.5. A notable feature of these growth accounting estimates is that the large advantage that France and West Germany held over the United Kingdom in terms of TFP growth during the Golden Age largely

Table 6.5 *Contributions to labour productivity growth, 1973–2007 (% per year)*

	Education	Capital per hour worked	TFP	Labour productivity growth
France				
1973–1995	0.2	1.2	1.5	2.9
1995–2007	0.3	0.7	0.9	1.9
Germany				
1973–1995	0.3	1.1	1.3	2.7
1995–2007	0.0	1.0	0.7	1.7
UK				
1973–1995	0.4	0.9	1.3	2.6
1995–2007	0.4	1.2	1.0	2.6
United States				
1973–1995	0.3	0.5	0.4	1.2
1995–2007	0.3	1.2	1.1	2.6

Note: Estimates are for the market sector.
Sources: 1973–1995: O'Mahony (1999); 1995–2007: van Ark (2011).
Education contributions from 1973 to 1995 are estimated based on years of schooling in Morrisson and Murtin (2009).

disappeared, and then was reversed in the next 40 years. In part, this reflected lower scope for catch-up in France and Germany as time went on but, it was also a result of relatively strong productivity growth in market services in the United Kingdom which carried a higher weight as these economies de-industrialized. Strikingly, after 1995, the capital deepening contribution to labour productivity growth in the United Kingdom exceeded that in Germany in the context of different rates of investment in ICT.

6.2 THE THATCHER EXPERIMENT

The policies of the Conservative government, led by Margaret Thatcher which took office in 1979, remain highly controversial. In many respects, they represented a sharp break with the earlier post-war period and this was certainly true of supply-side policies relevant to growth performance. Reforms of fiscal policy were made, including the restructuring of taxation by increasing VAT while reducing income tax rates and to restrain the growth of public expenditure, notably by indexing transfer payments to prices rather than wages, while aiming to restore a balanced budget. Industrial policy was downsized as subsidies were cut and privatization of state-owned businesses was embraced while deregulation, including most notably of financial markets with 'Big Bang' in 1986, was promoted. Legal reforms of industrial relations further reduced trade-union bargaining power which had initially been undermined by rising unemployment. In general, these changes were accepted rather than reversed by Labour after 1997.

In fact, before, during and after Thatcher, government policy moved in the direction of increasing competition in product markets. In particular, protectionism was discarded with liberalization through GATT negotiations, entry into the European Community in 1973, the retreat from industrial subsidies and foreign exchange controls in the Thatcher years and the implementation of the European Single Market legislation in the 1990s. It should be recognized that during the 1980s EU membership was an integral part of the Thatcher reform programme through its positive effects on competition, as is reflected in strong British support for the legislation to establish the European Single Market. The average effective rate of protection fell from 9.3 per cent in 1968 to 4.7 per cent in 1979, and 1.2 per cent in 1986 (Ennew et al., 1990), subsidies were reduced from £9bn (at 1980 prices) in 1969 to £5bn in 1979 and £0.3bn in 1990 (Wren, 1996a), and import penetration in manufacturing rose from 20.8 per cent in 1970 to 40.8 per cent by 2000. Trade liberalization in its various guises reduced price-cost margins (Hitiris, 1978; Griffith, 2001). The downward trend in the mark-up from the 1970s onwards appears to have intensified further after the early 1990s (Macallan et al., 2008). Rather surprisingly, an adequate reform of competition policy was delayed until the Blair government.

The Thatcher government saw itself as ending the trade unions' veto on economic policy reform and many of the changes of the 1980s would have been regarded as inconceivable by informed opinion in the 1960s and 1970s; this was the point at which the post-war consensus was abandoned.[3] Moreover, the early 1980s saw unemployment return to 1930s' levels (Boyer and Hatton, 2002) which conventional wisdom had thought incompatible with re-election. So, how was the government able to break out of the constraints imposed by the political economy of the previous three decades? The answer probably lies in a combination of the economic failures of the 1970s, the Falklands War, political strife in the Labour Party, and a maverick Prime Minister who over-rode the doubts of the risk-averse majority of her colleagues. It was not so much that the determinants of government popularity changed but rather that its underpinnings were different from the simplistic beliefs of the 1960s. Thus, the correct specification seems to have included the change in unemployment rather than its level, while perceived government competence in economic management and personal economic expectations were important (Price and Sanders, 1993; Sanders, 1996). The Falklands popularity boost was the icing on the cake in 1983 while in 1987 unemployment was falling and by then economic expectations were buoyant.

The implementation of supply-side policy reform was far from perfect but, on balance, improved productivity performance. Privatization which reduced the share of GDP supplied by state-owned enterprises from 12 per cent of GDP in 1979 to 2 per cent in 1997 is a case in point. The evidence is that while TFP in these businesses improved significantly during the process of privatization there was no lasting effect on trend TFP growth (Green and Haskel, 2004). The longer-term problem was the familiar one of weak competition and weak shareholders. It proved very difficult to replace competition as an antidote to principal–agent problems through price-cap regulation (Helm and Tindall, 2009). Nevertheless, the productivity

---

[3] In this context 'consensus' should be understood as a concept of the set of policies regarded as feasible by senior politicians and civil servants given presumed political constraints (cf. Kavanagh and Morris, 1994). This had implied a high degree of policy convergence but did not connote ideological convergence between the main political parties (Hickson, 2004).

Table 6.6 *Levels of productivity (UK = 100 in each year)*

	France	West Germany	USA
Y/HW, 1979			
Market sector	130	131	154
Manufacturing	133	147	190
Electricity, gas and water	166	158	301
Y/HW, 1996			
Market sector	132	129	121
Manufacturing	130	126	171
Electricity, gas and water	120	84	163
TFP, 1979			
Market sector	117	127	140
Manufacturing	118	133	168
Electricity, gas and water	92	119	170
TFP, 1995			
Market sector	108	115	119
Manufacturing	103	108	142
Electricity, gas and water	87	75	115

Source: O'Mahony (1999).

gap with the international peer group narrowed significantly between 1919 and 1995 (cf. Table 6.6).

Selective industrial policy fell out of favour. This was partly because the 1970s' experience led to disillusionment and partly because international treaties and, in particular, EU rules on state aid constrained policy. Whereas in 1981/6 state aid was 3.8 per cent of manufacturing GDP by 1994/6 this had fallen to 0.9 per cent. DTI expenditure on industrial policy measures was £421.4 million in 1997/8 (prior to devolution) of which £121.9 million went on science and technology schemes, £171.3 million for support for small firms and £128.2 million on regional policy (Wren, 2001). By 2006, virtually all (91 per cent) state aid was based on horizontal rather than selective policies (Buigues and Sekkat, 2011). The switch from selective to horizontal industrial policies was appropriate but the horizontal policies themselves were questionable in some respects. Areas of concern include education, infrastructure, innovation and regulation.

An important step forward was made in terms of the expansion of university education where the proportion of 18-year olds enrolling roughly tripled between the early 1980s and mid-1990s. On the other hand, cognitive skills as measured by international test scores had improved only marginally by the late 1990s (Woessmann, 2016) despite the introduction of the National Curriculum in 1988. The United Kingdom net stock of public capital relative to GDP, and to the stock of private capital, fell sharply between 1980 and 2000 (from 63.9 to 40.3 per cent and from 61.5 to 37.0 per cent, respectively) and rates of public investment implied that these ratios would continue to fall over the long run to a level that is clearly suboptimal. To maintain the level of public capital to GDP at a growth maximizing level, investment of about 2.7 per cent of GDP per year would be needed (Kamps, 2005) but in the late 1990s the United Kingdom invested only 1.7 per cent of GDP. R & D fell to below 2 per cent of GDP but the United Kingdom did not follow the example of the United States and introduce an R & D tax credit although analysis suggested that the policy might raise United Kingdom TFP growth by about 0.3 percentage points per year (Griffith et al., 2001). The United Kingdom remained a lightly regulated economy by European standards but productivity-inhibiting land-use planning rules remained or were even tightened. For example, planning policy, by making land for retailing very expensive and by constraining retailers to choose less productive sites, has reduced the level of TFP in supermarkets by about 32 per cent in post-1996 compared with pre-1988 stores thereby significantly reducing the rate of TFP growth in the sector (Cheshire et al., 2015).

The Thatcher period was notable for a shift from direct to indirect taxation as marginal rates of personal income tax were reduced, the standard rate to 25 per cent and the top rate to 40 per cent by 1988, while the standard VAT rate increased from 8 to 15 per cent in 1979 and then 17.5 per cent in 1991. The disincentive effects that worried Tanzi (1969) were mitigated. Nevertheless, it is fair to say that United

Kingdom policy was quite timid in making the sort of reforms that research suggests would be most effective in stimulating long-run growth. This could have entailed reducing the effective rate of corporate tax while extending the VAT base which remained very narrow by international standards (Owens and Whitehouse, 1996). The effective marginal rate of corporate tax actually rose steeply despite cuts in the headline rate as depreciation allowances were reduced (King and Robson, 1993).

The clear success story was the strengthening of competition. As an 'out-of-sample test', this reinforces the argument of Chapter 5 that weak competition undermined productivity performance in the Golden Age. Increased competition and openness in the later twentieth century went with better productivity performance. Proudman and Redding (1998) found that across British industry during 1970–1990 openness raised the rate of productivity convergence with the technological leader and, in a study looking at catch-up across European industries, Nicoletti and Scarpetta (2003) found that TFP growth was inversely related to PMR.[4] The implication of a lower PMR score as compared with France and Germany was a TFP growth advantage for the United Kingdom of about 0.5 percentage points per year in the 1990s. At the sectoral level, when concentration ratios fell in the United Kingdom in the 1980s, there was a strong positive impact on labour productivity growth (Haskel, 1991). Entry and exit accounted for an increasing proportion of manufacturing productivity growth, rising from 25 per cent in 1980–1985 to 40 per cent in 1995–2000 (Criscuolo et al., 2004).[5]

The impact was felt at least partly through greater pressure on management to perform, and through firm-worker bargains which raised effort and improved working practices. Increases in competition resulting from the European Single Market raised both the level

---

[4]   PMR is an acronym for 'product market regulation' and denotes an OECD index of the extent to which competition is inhibited by regulation.

[5]   This comes entirely from more entry and exit rather than a greater productivity impact from entry and exit, see Criscuolo et al. (2004, Table 2).

and growth rate of TFP in plants which were part of multi-plant firms and thus most prone to agency problems (Griffith, 2001). The 1980s saw a surge in productivity growth in unionized firms as organizational change took place under pressure of competition (Machin and Wadhwani, 1989) and de-recognition of unions, in the context of increases in foreign competition, had a strong effect on productivity growth in the late 1980s (Gregg et al., 1993). The negative impact of multi-unionism on TFP growth, apparent from the 1950s through the 1970s, evaporated after 1979 (Bean and Crafts, 1996).

The 1980s and 1990s saw major changes in the conduct and structure of British industrial relations. Trade union membership and bargaining power were seriously eroded. By 2001, only 19 per cent of private sector workers belonged to a trade union and the modal type was single unionism while collective bargaining covered only 30 per cent of private sector employees in 1998 (Gospel, 2005). Trade unions were recognized in only 24 per cent of workplaces in 1998 compared with 50 per cent in 1980 (Brown et al., 2008). Some of these changes were stimulated by increased competition in product markets and the associated reduction in the value of union membership. In addition, Conservative governments passed eight separate Acts whose cumulative effect was to end 'voluntarism' and remove most of the trade unions' legal immunities. Inter alia, this legislation ended the closed shop and secondary picketing, introduced secret ballots on strike action and imposed large penalties on unions who failed to comply (Wrigley, 2002). This last provision encouraged employers to use the law and injunctions became frequent. By the end of the century, the adverse impact of trade unionism on productivity performance had disappeared (Metcalf, 2005).

The separation of ownership and control in quoted companies became still more entrenched during the 1980s and early 1990s. Although the dispersion of share ownership was similar to that of 1950 (Franks et al., 2009), the percentage of shares held by domestic financial institutions continued to increase reaching a peak of 62 per cent in 1993. Institutional investors were well-known at this time for their passivity.[6] The evidence on share valuations indicates that they were also short-termist. Miles (1993) found that during the 1980s investors acted very myopically in terms of their discount rates and their unwillingness to give due weight to future cash flows. Moreover, the combination of short-termism and outside control tends to be persistent because unduly high discount rates mean a switch to inside control lowers the present value of the company (Morris, 1998). Given this short-termism, managers would rationally raise dividends at the expense of investment especially in projects with a long-term payoff, a strategy which reduced the risk of takeover (Dickerson et al., 1998).

Deregulation provided some amelioration of these problems, notably by improving the market for corporate control during the 1980s and 1990s. A key aspect of this was the advent of management buyouts often financed by private equity investors which was encouraged by relaxation of the rules on the financing of share buybacks. MBOs on average delivered large gains in TFP (Harris et al., 2005) and encouraged large ownership stakes for CEOs which addressed corporate governance problems. Private equity buyouts especially have delivered significant improvements in profitability and productivity (Toms et al., 2015). Nevertheless, the evidence is that the short-termism problem among quoted companies is still serious and has a significant adverse impact on investment (Davies et al., 2014) while management quality is still inferior to that in peer group countries such as Germany, Sweden and the United States (Bloom et al., 2016).

This review of the evidence suggests that Thatcherism was a partial solution to the problems which led to underperformance in the Golden Age, in particular, those which had arisen from weak competition. The reforms encouraged the effective diffusion of new technology rather than greater invention, and worked more through reducing inefficiency than promoting investment-led growth. Compared with the counterfactual of continuing with 1970s' policies, in terms of Figure 1.1, there was some improvement in the Schumpeter line but not the Solow

---

[6] For a full discussion of why institutional passivity was rational in the circumstances see Short and Keasey (2005).

Line. Of the two key institutional legacies, corporate governance remained a serious problem despite some amelioration but reform of the system of industrial relations was implemented quite effectively.

6.3 THE UNITED KINGDOM IN THE ICT REVOLUTION

Table 6.5 shows that after 1995 American labour productivity growth rebounded, the United Kingdom kept pace, but Germany slowed and was below the United Kingdom and the USA, as were most European countries. The acceleration in American productivity growth was underpinned by ICT. Since the main impact of ICT on economic growth comes through its use as a new form of capital equipment, the development of this new general purpose technology gave Europe a great opportunity to raise productivity growth, but most countries have been less successful in responding than the United States. However, the United Kingdom did benefit more than most, as is reflected in Table 6.7. ICT has had considerable potential to improve productivity growth in some service sectors, especially finance and distribution and relatively good productivity performance after 1995 has been based on a strong contribution from market services.

The diffusion of ICT has been aided by complementary investments in intangible capital and in high-quality human capital. Expansion of higher education has helped the United Kingdom but especially notable is a strong volume of investment in intangible capital (cf. Table 6.3). The international evidence is also that the diffusion of ICT has been significantly inhibited in countries which are heavily regulated (Cette and Lopez, 2012). Research at OECD indicates that restrictive product market regulation deterred investment in ICT capital directly (Conway et al., 2006) and the indirect effect of regulation in raising costs was relatively pronounced in sectors that use ICT intensively. Notably, employment protection has been shown to deter investment in ICT equipment (Gust and Marquez, 2004) because it increases the costs of reorganizing working practices and upgrading the labour force, which are central to realizing the productivity potential of ICT (Brynjolfsson and Hitt, 2003). Since

Table 6.7 *Labour productivity growth in the market sector, 1995–2007 (% per year)*
a) *Growth accounting*

	Labour quality	ICTK/ HW	Non-ICT K/HW	TFP	Labour productivity growth
UK	0.4	0.8	0.4	1.0	2.6
France	0.3	0.3	0.4	0.9	1.9
Germany	0.0	0.5	0.5	0.7	1.7
USA	0.3	0.9	0.3	1.1	2.6

b) *Sectoral contributions*

	ICT production	Goods production	Market services	Reallocation	Labour productivity growth
UK	0.5	0.7	1.6	–0.2	2.6
France	0.4	0.8	0.7	0.0	1.9
Germany	0.5	0.9	0.4	–0.1	1.7
USA	0.8	0.3	1.8	–0.3	2.6

Source: van Ark (2011).

these forms of regulation have weakened over time, the story is not that European regulation became more stringent but rather that existing regulation became more costly in the context of a new technological era.

For the United Kingdom, the 1980s' deregulation of services that are intensive in the use of ICT (notably finance and retailing), which reduced barriers to entry, was important for its relatively successful response to the new technology, as the OECD cross-country comparisons reveal.[7] It is also clear that investment in ICT is much more

---

[7] The sensitivity of productivity performance in retailing to regulation is underlined by the sharp reduction in TFP growth in this sector in the United Kingdom after the introduction of stricter limits on out-of-town supermarkets in 1996 (Haskel and Sadun, 2012).

profitable and has a bigger productivity payoff if it is accompanied by organizational change in working and management practices (Crespi et al., 2007). This would not have happened with 1970s-style industrial relations in conditions of weak competition. For example, Prais (1981, pp. 198–199) noted the egregious example of the news-paper industry where these conditions precluded the introduction of electronic equipment in Fleet Street although an investment of £50 million could have reduced costs by £35 million per year.

Putting this recent experience into longer-run perspective, three points deserve to be made. First, Britain has been relatively good at the diffusion of ICT in market services whereas in the earlier post-war period it was relatively bad at the diffusion of Fordist techniques in manufacturing. Second, ICT is a disruptive technology which requires quite radical changes in the ways companies operate if it is to be exploited well. This may help to promote faster adoption of ICT in LMEs rather than CMEs given the greater flexibility and greater reliance on college education of the former compared with the latter. Taken together, these points suggest that relative social capability varies according to the technological epoch. Third, success in ICT diffusion was an unintended consequence of the deregulation and resistance to further pursuit of corporatism in the Thatcher period.

6.4 IMPLICATIONS OF THE FINANCIAL CRISIS

On the eve of the crisis, the growth performance of the United Kingdom economy was generally seen as quite satisfactory (Van Reenen, 2013). A long period of relative economic decline vis-à-vis other European economies seemed to have come to an end under the auspices of the supply-side policies initiated under the Thatcher government, and con-tinued in most respects by New Labour. Subsequent developments during the financial crisis and its aftermath have come as a rude shock. Labour productivity growth over the period 2007–2016 was just 0.09 per cent per year and growth of real GDP per person was only 0.19 per cent per year, in each case at least 2 percentage points below the rates achieved in 1995–2007 (cf. Table 6.2).

In the context of an optimistic account of late twentieth century British economic growth, the early twenty-first century productivity slowdown raises several related questions. Was pre-2007 growth performance unsustainable? Is slow growth post-2007 mainly a result of the financial crisis? Does the very fact of the crisis imply that seemingly decent growth was actually a 'mirage'?

The Office for Budget Responsibility believes that the trend rate of labour productivity growth continues to be 2.2 per cent per year, i.e., more or less what was achieved pre-crisis. A less-optimistic interpretation might be that the average productivity growth rate of 2.1 per cent per year over the period 1995–2007 was a bit above the medium-term trend rate at the end of the period. Nevertheless, there is every reason to think that growth of output per hour worked around 1.5 to 1.75 per cent per year was sustainable – enough to keep pace with the major European economies and way ahead of the actual rate since 2007.

When Labour won a landslide victory in the 1997 election, it was possible to wonder whether in government it would revert to 'Old Labour' policies. The answer soon became apparent and was a resounding 'No'. 1970s-style policy was conspicuous by its absence: there was no nationalization programme, no move to subsidize manufacturing investment, no counterpart of the National Enterprise Board, no return to high marginal rates of direct tax, no attempt to resist de-industrialization by supporting declining industries and no major reversal of industrial relations reform. Implicitly, the Thatcher supply-side reforms had been accepted. The changes that Labour made were to strengthen some aspects of horizontal industrial policies with a new emphasis on education, R & D, investing in public capital and strengthening competition policy. There was a strong element of continuity in supply-side policy in terms of strengths (competition, regulation), weaknesses (innovation, infrastructure) and areas where further improvement was desirable (education, tax system). There is no reason to think growth was being undermined by policy errors.

The economy probably had a small positive output gap in 2007 but not big enough seriously to distort perceptions of pre-crisis performance.[8] It can fairly be pointed out that a more heavily regulated and somewhat smaller financial services sector may well contribute less to productivity growth in future than in the pre-crisis years but, it is not correct to see its pre-crisis contribution as a mirage.[9] It is also apparent that productivity growth weakened somewhat after 2003 to a pre-crisis average of about 1.7 per cent per year compared with 2.6 per cent per year in the previous five years.

It is well-known that financial crises can have permanent adverse direct effects on the level of potential output. Thinking in terms of a production function or growth accounting, there may be direct adverse effects on capital inputs as investment is interrupted, on human capital if skills are lost, on labour inputs through increases in equilibrium unemployment and on TFP if R & D is cut back or if innovative firms cannot get finance. The transition period while the levels effect materializes and during which growth rates are depressed may be quite long. Moreover, recovery is often slow; Reinhart and Rogoff (2014) estimated that the median length of time before real GDP per person returns to its pre-crisis level is 6.5 years.

This could imply that recent labour productivity performance basically reflects a large levels effect resulting from the financial crisis but does not imply that long-term trend growth has been reduced, in which case log labour productivity would maintain a trend path parallel to what would have been expected in 2007.[10] Oulton and Sebastia-Barrel (2017) found a long-run impact on the level of labour

---

[8] The output gap is always measured with difficulty but the best guess is that it was about 2 per cent in 2007 according to the detailed analysis in Murray (2014).

[9] It is sometimes claimed that mismeasurement of financial services output distorted the pre-crisis picture; Oulton (2013) shows that any such effect is very small – at most 0.1 per cent per year during 2000–2007. According to the EUKLEMS database, output per hour worked grew at 4.23 per cent per year between 1997 and 2007 and, weighted by the sector's value-added share, contributed 0.19 per cent per year to total labour productivity growth.

[10] This would actually be quite similar to what analysis based on time-series econometrics suggests for the experience of the United States in the context of the massive financial crisis during the Great Depression (Ben-David et al., 2003).

productivity of 1.1 per cent per year that the crisis lasts. There is good reason to think that the crisis also had significant temporary effects on productivity performance which may not yet have completely evaporated. Exit of low productivity firms has been slowed down by a period of exceptionally low interest rates.[11] Misallocation of labour appears to have been a key issue as new hires and employment growth have been disproportionately concentrated in low productivity sectors with an impact estimated to account for as much as two-thirds of the shortfall in labour productivity compared with a pre-crisis projection (Patterson et al., 2016).

Banking crises reflect market failures in the banking sector combined with a failure of regulation to address them effectively. The problems arise from moral hazard and coordination failures in a context of asymmetric information. The typical pre-crisis symptom is rapid expansion of credit coupled with excessive risk-taking. The likelihood of bank failures increases as leverage goes up and the ratio of equity capital to assets falls. Banking crises happen even in economies with very strong growth fundamentals if banks are badly regulated and under-capitalized. The classic example is the United States where about a third of all banks failed in the years 1929–1933 but nevertheless, as was noted in Chapter 4, TFP growth in the 1930s was impressive.

The financial crisis of 2007–2008 in the United Kingdom matches this familiar pattern. Regulation was deficient and leverage soared following the deregulation of the 1980s with the median ratio of total assets to shareholder claims increasing from around 20 in the 1970s to almost 50 at the pre-crisis peak (ICB, 2011). In effect, there was a huge implicit subsidy to risk-taking by banks that were too big to fail and were allowed to operate with inadequate equity capital. This was a major failure of the policy reforms undertaken in the 1980s. That said, it should not be inferred that pre-crisis growth was

[11] A Bank-of-England simulation suggests that had normal interest rates prevailed, the level of overall labour productivity would have been 2 or even possibly 3 per cent higher (Haldane, 2017).

predicated on unsound finance even though the cost of capital would have been higher with resilient bank balance sheets. Miles et al. (2013) offer an illustrative calculation which suggests that the lower capital intensity entailed by the introduction of appropriate capital-adequacy regulation would have reduced the level of GDP by about 0.2 per cent.

In sum, the financial crisis does not imply that pre-crisis growth was somehow illusory. The crisis was a result of inadequate financial regulation rather than weak productivity performance. The shock of the near collapse of the banking system has led to a 'lost decade' in terms of economic growth but it is too soon to tell what its implications for future long-term trend growth will be.

6.5 CONCLUSIONS

After the Golden Age, the United Kingdom's relative growth performance improved. United Kingdom productivity growth was slower than pre-1973 but growth in other countries fell by more. The contributions to productivity growth from capital deepening and TFP were now similar or slightly better than in France and Germany rather than significantly worse. A notable success for the United Kingdom was its rapid adoption of ICT which played to its strengths in human capital and light-touch regulation.

The reforms of the Thatcher government were a radical response to the poor performance of the United Kingdom economy during the 1970s. The general thrust was to improve the functioning of a struggling LME. The big success stories were the strengthening of competition and the ending of the trade union veto on supply-side policies. Reductions in high marginal income tax rates, the downsizing of selective industrial policy and the expansion of college education were other notable positives. On the other hand, infrastructure and innovation policies left a lot to be desired. With regard to the institutional legacies of the early start, the industrial relations problem which had seemed intractable during the 1970s was largely neutralized, but the separation of ownership and control continued to be problematic, as witnessed by the short-termism of investors.

The financial crisis in 2007 brought an end to a long period of respectable growth. The crisis should not be taken as evidence that this growth was unsustainable but as an indictment of a policy framework that paid too little attention to financial stability. The impact of the crisis on productivity growth was severe and protracted and far exceeded the relatively modest slowdown of the last years before the crisis. Better regulation of the banking system could have averted the crisis without undermining growth.

7 Concluding Comments

Detailed conclusions have been presented at the end of each chapter and they will not be repeated here. Rather, this is the opportunity to reflect on the big picture and to be a bit provocative. I want to review some lessons, both about analysing economic growth performance and about designing policy conducive to economic growth, which I take from the historical account in earlier chapters. Then, I wish to elaborate my (idiosyncratic) hypothesis about the implications of the 'early start', namely, that its adverse impact was felt most strongly during the Golden Age of economic growth after the Second World War.

The key to evaluating growth performance is, not surprisingly, to establish suitable reference points which underpin an assessment of how much changed and what was feasible. Of course, this has to be based on an adequate database that facilitates inter-temporal and international comparisons but it also requires an analytic framework based on growth economics. An important aspect of this is growth accounting which provides useful diagnostics. These points are exemplified by my discussion of the Industrial Revolution. Estimates of the rate of economic growth show that there was a notable acceleration in the late eighteenth and early nineteenth century which produced sustained economic growth in the face of considerable demographic pressure. This was unprecedented. However, by later standards the rate of economic growth was unimpressive and TFP growth was quite modest even though new technologies, notably including steam power, came along. Recognition of the limitations of the Industrial-Revolution economy provides an important context for later relative growth performance.

International comparisons offer benchmarks which guard against misleading interpretations based on a parochial assessment of performance. The interwar period provides a good example. For a while a quite optimistic view, especially of the 1930s, prevailed. The statistical basis for this was an account of United Kingdom productivity performance through time which described a U-shaped curve with the low point in Edwardian times and a revival between the wars. Compared with outcomes in the United States, however, TFP growth in the United Kingdom was increasingly disappointing. The acceleration in American TFP growth was about three times larger. The gap between the United Kingdom and the USA in levels of labour productivity in manufacturing actually increased during the 1930s even though the impact of the depression was much more damaging on the other side of the Atlantic.

Comparisons of levels of productivity or real GDP per person between countries rely on estimates of the purchasing power parity exchange rate. Inevitably, there are significant index-number problems in any such calculations which are, of course, central to the notion of relative economic decline which is the focal point of this book. They are, however, an essential ingredient of an evaluation of economic growth in the United Kingdom and the development of a database of purchasing-power-parity adjusted estimates of GDP per person for OECD countries by Angus Maddison has had a profound effect. This is especially clear in the context of the Golden Age of the 1950s through the early 1970s. Apologists for United Kingdom growth performance in this period used to point to a higher growth rate than in any other period and dismiss faster growth elsewhere in Europe as simply a reflection of an initial productivity shortfall and greater scope for catch-up. This loses all credibility, however, once it is recognized that the United Kingdom had been overtaken by much of its European peer group and had a lower real income level than they did by the end of the Golden Age.

In understanding the reasons for success and failure in economic growth, it is essential to examine incentive structures which result from institutions and government policies and which impact on investment and innovation. It has become widely agreed among both economic historians and economists that institutions matter for economic growth. This is, of course, substantiated by United Kingdom experience. The Industrial Revolution itself was predicated on an adequate set of institutions which were already in place including a strong state which could provide essential public goods and underpin a functioning market economy but was not above the law.

A key aspect of British economic history is that its long-run institutional trajectory was to arrive at a Liberal Market Economy (LME) rather than a Co-ordinated Market Economy (CME) destination in the second half of the twentieth century. In general, this meant a somewhat lower volume of investment and less patient capital than would be expected in a CME although perhaps having a compensating advantage in allowing flexible responses to shocks. The United Kingdom was disadvantaged during the Golden Age, which was the heyday of the CME as a configuration well suited to exploiting the opportunity for rapid catch-up growth from a starting point well behind the United States. On the other hand, when the ICT revolution came along, the United Kingdom was favoured by having the flexibility of an LME.

Economic historians often stress that institutions are persistent and this means that 'history matters'. Institutional reform is often difficult even when existing arrangements have plainly become dysfunctional – switching costs are high and the resistance of supporters of the status quo is hard to overcome. The longevity of the 'British system of industrial relations' during the twentieth century is a prime example. An implication of persistence is that growth performance can be affected by institutional legacies. At the same time, it is important to recognize that history also matters through its legacy of constraints on the policy choices of vote-seeking politicians.

Sometimes constraints have been the result of the arithmetic of winners and losers from a proposed policy change. An obvious example of this is the opposition to tariff reform in the early twentieth century where the structural changes linked to precocious industrialization worked against the protectionists and the United Kingdom was something of an outlier in its sustained commitment to free trade. In other cases, the legacy effect works through 'rules' which have been put in place intentionally to take away political discretion – for example, the commitment to balanced budgets in peacetime prior to the Second World War. The strongest constraints can, however, arise simply from 'inescapable' historical experience which promotes a policy paradigm. Thus, in the Golden Age, the 'post-war consensus' (or set of feasible policy choices) was anchored by the political imperative of no return to the perceived failures of the 1930s.

An important lesson from the history of economic growth is that supply-side policy can make a significant difference, as new growth economics suggests. The most obvious manifestation of this was during the Golden Age when many unfortunate policies were implemented and growth was undermined. Inter alia, there were big problems with industrial policy, control of nationalized industries, design of taxation and policy towards European economic integration. Perhaps, however, the biggest lesson to take from this experience is that competition policy (broadly defined) really matters for productivity performance in an LME. These were errors from inappropriate intervention but there have also been failures to intervene, with a persistent problem being lack of support for civil R & D.

An unfortunate implication of this discussion is that 'government failure' has been a serious problem. There are many reasons for this some of which have already been explained. At bottom, the key point is that, generally speaking, there are few votes to be gained from effective long-termist policies to promote productivity. The silver lining to this cloud is that, provided we don't forget, at least we know a lot about 'what doesn't work'.

The period of most acute relative economic decline was the 1950s, 1960s and 1970s. This was a period of rapid economic growth during which the United Kingdom failed fully to exploit the opportunity and was overtaken by many European economies including

France and West Germany. The main thrust of my argument, simply put, is that growth in the United Kingdom was undermined to a significant extent by institutional legacies which can be traced back to the early start and which interacted with weak competition in product markets to impair productivity performance.

In earlier chapters, I have outlined the evolution from the Industrial Revolution to the Golden Age of key institutions, namely, the systems of industrial relations and corporate governance, with a distinctive British flavour. These institutions developed along trajectories from which it turned out that it was difficult to escape. Their disadvantages became clear in the context of a malfunctioning LME after the Second World War.

The British system of industrial relations stemmed from the craft unionism of the nineteenth century. It was characterized by strong but decentralized collective bargaining in which union bargaining power was underpinned by legal immunities. Workers engaged in rent sharing which paid a wage premium and/or accepted low effort bargains. The switching costs of reforming industrial relations were seen as too high both by employers and politicians. The corporate governance of publicly quoted companies was characterized by an unusually high degree of separation of ownership and control with diffuse shareholding, that is, outside rather than inside control and equity rather than bank finance. This pattern was already visible in embryonic fashion in the nineteenth century but was intensified by the transition from personal to institutional shareholding. Short-termism consolidated outside control.

These institutional arrangements had a potential downside for productivity outcomes. In a world of asymmetric information, the separation of ownership and control implied that managers had considerable scope to underperform or to pursue objectives other than profit maximization, especially if competition was weak. Strong competition is an antidote to these principal-agent problems because it reduces the scope for managerial discretion and also makes it easier for shareholders to detect and act upon underperformance. Multi-unionism encouraged short-termism by workers and exacerbated the hold-up problems entailed in sunk-costs investment. When bargaining power of unions is strong, bolstered by legal privileges and tight labour markets, it might be expected that a significant share of profits are diverted to workers including through the acceptance of restrictive working practices. Competition addresses these problems by reducing the surplus that is available for unions to extract.

The early post-war decades were a period when competition in much of the economy was weaker than ever before in the context of protectionism, delayed entry into the EEC, regulation, nationalization and a largely ineffective competition policy. This configuration meant that the potential adverse effects on productivity of the institutional legacies of the early start materialized to a much greater extent.

A further implication of these institutions is that they were incompatible with the so-called 'Eichengreen cooperative equilibrium' with wage restraint in return for high investment. In general, this is more likely to be sustained in a CME. The key to maintaining the bargain is that both sides apply a low discount rate to future payoffs. The short-termism endemic in the United Kingdom's distinctive institutions was not conducive to patience. This accelerated relative economic decline given that other European countries did achieve rapid catch-up growth in the Golden Age through a corporatist approach.

Finally, it should be remembered that the Golden Age can be seen as the high point of the restricted set of policy choices consistent with the 'post-war consensus'. This was profoundly affected by the experience of persistent high unemployment in the interwar period and the structure of industrial relations. In particular, the political imperative after the Second World War was to maintain a very low level of unemployment. Strong but decentralized collective bargaining potentially made this problematic, as subsequent experience confirmed only too well. Accordingly, supply-side policy was designed with a view to making it acceptable to trade union leaders in the hope that this would be reciprocated by wage restraint and, in effect, the

NAIRU would be held down. This precluded important reforms including, of course, to industrial relations.

The discussion of this chapter, and indeed the whole book, relies fundamentally on the ideas and techniques of modern economics and the evidence base that has developed based on these foundations. This seems appropriate for an interpretation of the United Kingdom experience of economic growth over the past 250 years. Even so, the learning process between economic history and economics should be a two-way street. In this respect, economic historians have to describe the contours of growth and communicate them to economists. More than that, however, they have to explain how and why 'history matters' in the sense that in various ways the past constrains growth performance. My narrative has tried to achieve both these objectives and thus to show the value of a long-run historical perspective in thinking about economic growth.

References

Abramovitz, M. (1986), 'Catching Up, Forging Ahead, and Falling Behind', *Journal of Economic History*, **46**, 385–406.

Abramovitz, M. and David, P. A. (1996), 'Convergence and Deferred Catch-Up: Productivity Leadership and the Waning of American Exceptionalism', in R. Landau, T. Taylor and G. Wright (eds.), *The Mosaic of Economic Growth*. Stanford, CA: Stanford University Press, 21–62.

(2001), 'Two Centuries of American Macroeconomic Growth: From Exploitation of Resource Abundance to Knowledge-Driven Development', Stanford Institute for Economic Policy Research Discussion Paper No. 01–05.

Acemoglu, D. (1998), 'Why Do New Technologies Complement Skills? Directed Technical Change and Wage Inequality', *Quarterly Journal of Economics*, **113**, 1055–1089.

(2002), 'Directed Technical Change', *Review of Economic Studies*, **69**, 781–809.

(2010), 'When Does Labor Scarcity Encourage Innovation?' *Journal of Political Economy*, **118**, 1037–1076.

Acheson, G. G., Campbell, G., Turner, J. D. and Vanteeva, N. (2015), 'Corporate Ownership and Control in Victorian Britain', *Economic History Review*, **68**, 911–936.

Aghion, P., Dewatripont, M. and Rey, P. (1997), 'Corporate Governance, Competition Policy and Industrial Policy', *European Economic Review*, **41**, 797–805.

Aghion, P. and Howitt, P. (1998), *Endogenous Growth Theory*. Cambridge, MA: MIT Press.

(2006), 'Appropriate Growth Theory: A Unifying Framework', *Journal of the European Economic Association*, **4**, 269–314.

Aldcroft, D. H. and Oliver, M. J. (2000), *Trade Unions and the Economy: 1870–2000*. Aldershot: Ashgate Publishing.

Allen, R. C. (2009a), *The British Industrial Revolution in Global Perspective*. Cambridge: Cambridge University Press.

(2009b), 'Engels' Pause: Technical Change, Capital Accumulation, and Inequality in the British Industrial Revolution', *Explorations in Economic History*, **46**, 418–435.

(2012), 'Technology and the Great Divergence: Global Economic Development Since 1820', *Explorations in Economic History*, **49**, 1–16.

Andrews, P. W. S. and Brunner, E. (1950), 'Productivity and the Businessman', *Oxford Economic Papers*, **2**, 197–225.

Badinger, H. (2005), 'Growth Effects of Economic Integration: Evidence from the EU Member States', *Review of World Economics*, **141**, 50–78.

Bairoch, P. (1982), 'International Industrialisation Levels from 1750 to 1980', *Journal of European Economic History*, **11**, 269–331.

(1991), 'The City and Technological Innovation', in P. Higonet, D. Landes and H. Rosovsky (eds.), *Favorites of Fortune*. Cambridge, MA: Harvard University Press, 159–176.

Bakker, G., Crafts, N. and Woltjer, P. (2017), 'A Vision of the Growth Process in a Technologically Progressive Economy', University of Warwick CAGE Working Paper No. 341.

Baldwin, R. E. and Robert-Nicoud, F. (2007), 'Entry and Asymmetric Lobbying: Why Governments Pick Losers', *Journal of the European Economic Association*, **5**, 1064–1093.

Baliga, S. and Polak, B. (2004), 'The Emergence and Persistence of the Anglo-Saxon and German Financial Systems', *Review of Financial Studies*, **17**, 129–163.

Bamberg, J. H. (1988), 'The Rationalisation of the British Cotton Industry in the Interwar Years', *Textile History*, **19**, 83–102.

Barro, R. J. (1999), 'Notes on Growth Accounting', *Journal of Economic Growth*, **4**, 119–137.

Bean, C. and Crafts, N. (1996), 'British Economic Growth Since 1945: Relative Economic Decline ... and Renaissance?' in N. Crafts and G. Toniolo (eds.), *Economic Growth in Europe Since 1945*. Cambridge: Cambridge University Press, 131–172.

Ben-David, D., Lumsdaine, R. and Papell, D. H. (2003), 'Unit Roots, Postwar Slowdowns and Long-Run Growth: Evidence from Two Structural Breaks', *Empirical Economics*, **28**, 303–319.

Berrill, K. (1960), 'International Trade and the Rate of Economic Growth', *Economic History Review*, **12**, 351–359.

Blanchflower, D., Oswald, A. and Sanley, P. (1996), 'Wages, Profits, and Rent-Sharing', *Quarterly Journal of Economics*, **111**, 227–252.

Bloom, N. and van Reenen, J. (2007), 'Measuring and Explaining Management Practices Across Firms and Countries', *Quarterly Journal of Economics*, **122**, 1351–1408.

Bloom, N., Safun, R. and van Reenen, J. (2016), 'Management as a Technology', CEPR Discussion Paper No. 11312.

Booth, A. (1987), 'Britain in the 1930s: A Managed Economy', *Economic History Review*, **40**, 499–522.

Bowden, S. M. (1991), 'Demand and Supply Constraints in the Interwar UK Car Industry: Did the Manufacturers Get It Right?' *Business History*, **33**, 241–267.

Boyer, G. R. and Hatton, T. J. (2002), 'New Estimates of British Unemployment, 1870–1913', *Journal of Economic History*, **62**, 643–675.

Bretherton, R. F., Burchardt, F. A. and Rutherford, R. S. G. (1941), *Public Investment and the Trade Cycle in Great Britain*. Oxford: Clarendon Press.

British Parliamentary Papers (1940), *Report of the Royal Commission on the Distribution of the Industrial Population*, Cmnd. 6153.

British Parliamentary Papers (1944), *Employment Policy After the War*. Cmnd. 6527.

Broadberry, S. N. (1994), 'Why Was Unemployment in Post-war Britain So Low?' *Bulletin of Economic Research*, **46**, 241–261.

(1997), *The Productivity Race*. Cambridge: Cambridge University Press.

(1998), 'How Did the United States and Germany Overtake Britain? A Sectoral Analysis of Comparative Productivity Levels', *Journal of Economic History*, **58**, 375–407.

(2003), 'Human Capital and Productivity Performance: Britain, the United States and Germany, 1870–1990', in P. A. David and M. Thomas (eds.), *The Economic Future in Historical Perspective*. Oxford: Oxford University Press, 103–133.

Broadberry, S. N. (2006), *Market Services and the Productivity Race, 1850–2000*. Cambridge: Cambridge University Press.

(2013), 'Accounting for the Great Divergence', paper presented to conference on 'Long Run Growth: Unified Growth Theory and Economic History', University of Warwick.

Broadberry, S. N., Campbell, B. and van Leeuwen, B. (2013), 'When Did Britain Industrialise? The Sectoral Distribution of the Labour Force and Labour Productivity in Britain, 1381–1851', *Explorations in Economic History*, **50**, 16–27.

Broadberry, S. N., Campbell, B., Klein, A., Overton, M. and van Leeuwen, B. (2015), *British Economic Growth, 1270–1870*. Cambridge: Cambridge University Press.

Broadberry, S. N. and Crafts, N. (1990), 'The Implications of British Macroeconomic Policy in the 1930s for Long-Run Growth Performance', *Rivista di Storia Economica*, 7, 1–19.

(1992), 'Britain's Productivity Gap in the 1930s: Some Neglected Factors', *Journal of Economic History*, **52**, 531–558.

(1996), 'British Economic Policy and Industrial Performance in the Early Postwar Period', *Business History*, **38**, 65–91.

Broadberry, S. and Crafts, N. (2001), 'Competition and Innovation in 1950s Britain', *Business History*, **43**, 97–118.

Broadberry, S. and Marrison, A. (2002), 'External Economies of Scale in the Lancashire Cotton Industry, 1900–1950', *Economic History Review*, **55**, 51–77.

Broadberry, S. and O'Mahony, M. (2007), 'Britain's Twentieth-Century Productivity Performance in International Perspective', in N. Crafts, I. Gazeley and A. Newell (eds.), *Work and Pay in Twentieth-Century Britain*. Oxford: Oxford University Press, 301–329.

Brown, W., Bryson, A. and Forth, J. (2008), 'Competition and the Retreat from Collective Bargaining', National Institute of Economic and Social Research Discussion Paper No. 318.

Brynjolfsson, E. and Hitt, L. (2003), 'Computing Productivity: Firm-Level Evidence', *Review of Economics and Statistics*, **85**, 793–808.

Buigues, P. A. and Sekkat, K. (2011), 'Public Subsidies to Business: An International Comparison', *Journal of Industry, Competition and Trade*, **11**, 1–24.

Bulpitt, J. and Burnham, P. (1999), 'Operation Robot and the British Political Economy in the Early-1950s: The Politics of Market Strategies', *Contemporary British History*, **13**, 1–31.

Burgess, K. (1975), *The Origins of British Industrial Relations*. London: Croom Helm.

Byrne, D. M., Oliner, S. D. and Sichel, D. E. (2013), 'Is the Information Technology Revolution Over?' *International Productivity Monitor*, **25**, 20–36.

Cain, L. P. and Paterson, D. G. (1986), 'Biased Technical Change, Scale, and Factor Proportions in American Industry, 1850–1919', *Journal of Economic History*, **46**, 153–164.

Cain, P. (1988), 'Railways, 1870–1914: The Maturity of the Private System', in M. Freeman and D. H. Aldcroft (eds.), *Transport in Victorian Britain*. Manchester: Manchester University Press, 93–133.

Cameron, G. and Wallace, C. (2002), 'Macroeconomic Performance in the Bretton Woods Era and After', *Oxford Review of Economic Policy*, **18**, 479–494.

Campbell, G. and Turner, J. D. (2011), 'Substitutes for Legal Protection: Corporate Governance and Dividends in Victorian Britain', *Economic History Review*, **64**, 571–597.

Carlin, W. and Soskice, D. (2006), *Macroeconomics: Imperfections, Institutions and Policies*. Oxford: Oxford University Press.

Carter, S. B., Gartner, S. S., Haines, M. R., Olmstead, A. L., Sutch, R. and Wright, G. (eds.) (2006), *Historical Statistics of the United States: Earliest Times to the Present*. Cambridge: Cambridge University Press.

Cassis, Y. (2006), *Capitals of Capital*. Cambridge: Cambridge University Press.

Cette, G. and Lopez, J. (2012), 'ICT Demand Behaviour: An International Comparison', *Economics of Innovation and New Technology*, **21**, 397–410.

Chabot, B. R. and Kurz, C. J. (2010), 'That's Where the Money Was: Foreign Bias and English Investment Abroad, 1866–1907', *Economic Journal*, **120**, 1056–1079.

Chambers, D. (2014), 'The City and the Corporate Economy Since 1870', in R. Floud, J. Humphries and P. Johnson (eds.), *The Cambridge Economic History of Modern Britain*, vol. **2**. Cambridge: Cambridge University Press, 255–278.

Cheffins, B. R. (2008), *Corporate Ownership and Control: British Business Transformed*. Oxford: Oxford University Press.

Cheffins, B. R., Koustas, D. K. and Chambers, D. (2013), 'Ownership Dispersion and the London Stock Exchange's 'Two-Thirds Rule': An Empirical Test', *Business History*, **55**, 670–693.

Cheshire, P. C., Hilber, C. A. L. and Kaplanis, I. (2015), 'Land-Use Regulation and Productivity – Land Matters: Evidence from a UK Supermarket Chain', *Journal of Economic Geography*, **22**, 43–73.

Ciliberto, F. (2010), 'Were British Cotton Entrepreneurs Technologically Backward?: Firm-Based Evidence on the Adoption of Ring Spinning', *Explorations in Economic History*, **47**, 487–504.

Clark, G. (1987), 'Why Isn't the Whole World Developed? Lessons from the Cotton Mills', *Journal of Economic History*, **47**, 141–173.

Clarke, R. (1985), *Industrial Economics*. Oxford: Blackwell.

Clarke, R., Davies, S. and Driffield, N. (1998), *Monopoly Policy in the UK: Assessing the Evidence*. Cheltenham: Edward Elgar.

Cochrane, S. (2009), 'Explaining London's Dominance in International Financial Services, 1870–1913', University of Oxford Department of Economics Discussion Paper No. 455.

Conway, P., de Rosa, D., Nicoletti, G. and Steiner, F. (2006), 'Regulation, Competition and Productivity Convergence', OECD Economics Department Working Paper No. 509.

Corti, G. (1976), 'Perspectives on Public Corporations and Public Enterprises in Five Nations', *Annals of Collective Economy*, **47**, 47–86.

Cowan, R. (1990), 'Nuclear Power Reactors: A Study in Technological Lock-In', *Journal of Economic History*, **50**, 541–567.

Coyle, C. and Turner, J. D. (2013), 'Law, Politics, and Financial Development: The Great Reversal of the UK Corporate Debt Market', *Journal of Economic History*, **73**, 810–846.

Crafts, N. (1984), 'Patterns of Economic Development in Nineteenth Century Europe', *Oxford Economic Papers* (1984), **36**, 438–458.

(1985), *British Economic Growth During the Industrial Revolution*. Oxford: Clarendon Press.

(1987), 'Long Term Unemployment in Britain in the 1930s', *Economic History Review*, **40**, 418–432.

(1989), 'Revealed Comparative Advantage in Manufacturing, 1899–1950', *Journal of European Economic History* (1989), **18**, 127–137.

(1995), 'Exogenous or Endogenous Growth: The Industrial Revolution Reconsidered', *Journal of Economic History*, **55**, 745–772.

(1998), 'Forging Ahead and Falling Behind: The Rise and Relative Decline of the First Industrial Nation', *Journal of Economic Perspectives*, **12**(2), 193–210.

(2002), 'The Solow Productivity Paradox in Historical Perspective', CEPR Discussion Paper No. 3142.

(2004a), 'Productivity Growth in the Industrial Revolution: A New Growth Accounting Perspective', *Journal of Economic History*, **64**, 521–535.

(2004b), 'Steam as General Purpose Technology: A Growth Accounting Perspective', *Economic Journal*, **114**, 338–351.

(2005), 'The First Industrial Revolution: Resolving the Slow Growth/Rapid Industrialization Paradox', *Journal of the European Economic Association*, **3**, 525–534.

(2009), 'Solow and Growth Accounting: A Perspective from Quantitative Economic History', *History of Political Economy*, **41**(5), 200–220.

(2011), 'Explaining the First Industrial Revolution: Two Views', *European Review of Economic History*, **15**, 153–168.

(2012), 'British Relative Economic Decline Revisited: The Role of Competition', *Explorations in Economic History*, **49**, 17–29.

(2013), 'Returning to Growth: Policy Lessons from History', *Fiscal Studies*, **34**, 255–282.

(2014), 'Walking Wounded: The British Economy in the Aftermath of World War I'. www.voxeu.org/article/walking-wounded-british-economy-aftermath-world-war-i

(2016), 'The Growth Effects of EU Membership for the UK: A Review of the Evidence', University of Warwick CAGE Working Paper No. 280.

Crafts, N. and Harley, C. K. (2004), 'Precocious British Industrialisation: A General Equilibrium Perspective', in L. Prados de la Escosura (ed.), *Exceptionalism and*

Industrialisation: Britain and Its European Rivals, 1688–1815. Cambridge: Cambridge University Press, 86–107.

Crafts, N. and Leunig, T. (2005), *The Historical Significance of Transport for Economic Growth and Productivity,* analytical evidence paper for the Eddington Transport Study. http://collections.europarchiv.org/tna/19200701291225

Crafts, N., Leunig, T. and Mulatu, A. (2008), 'Were British Railway Companies Well-Managed in the Early Twentieth Century?' *Economic History Review,* **61**, 842–866

Crafts, N., Leybourne, S. J. and Mills, T. C. (1989), 'The Climacteric in Late-Victorian Britain and France: A Re-appraisal of the Evidence', *Journal of Applied Econometrics,* **4**, 103–117.

Crafts, N. and Magnani, M. (2013), 'The Golden Age and the Second Globalization in Italy', in G. Toniolo (ed.), *The Oxford Handbook of the Italian Economy Since Unification.* Oxford: Oxford University Press, 69–107.

Crafts, N. and Mills, T. C. (2004), 'Was 19th-Century British Growth Steam-Powered? The Climacteric Revisited', *Explorations in Economic History,* **41**, 156–171.

(2005), 'TFP Growth in British and German Manufacturing, 1950–1996', *Economic Journal,* **115**, 649–670.

(2013), 'Rearmament to the Rescue? New Estimates of the Impact of Keynesian Policies in 1930s' Britain', *Journal of Economic History,* **73**, 1077–1104.

Crafts, N. and Mulatu, A. (2006), 'How Did the Location of Industry Respond to Falling Transport Costs in Britain Before World War I?' *Journal of Economic History,* **66**, 575–607.

Crafts, N. and Thomas, M. (1986), 'Comparative Advantage in UK Manufacturing Trade, 1910–1935', *Economic Journal,* **96**, 629–645.

Crafts, N. and Toniolo, G. (2008), 'European Economic Growth, 1950–2005: An Overview', CEPR Discussion Paper No. 6863.

Crespi, G., Criscuolo, C. and Haskel, J. (2007), 'Information Technology, Organizational Change and Productivity Growth: Evidence from UK Firms', London School of Economics Centre for Economic Performance Discussion Paper No. 783.

Criscuolo, C., Haskel, J. and Martin, R. (2004), 'Import Competition, Productivity and Restructuring in UK Manufacturing', *Oxford Review of Economic Policy,* **20**, 393–408.

Crouch, C. (1993), *Industrial Relations and European State Traditions.* Oxford: Clarendon Press.

Cusack, T., Iversen, T. and Soskice, D. (2007), 'Economic Interests and the Origins of Electoral Systems', *American Political Science Review,* **101**, 373–391.

(2010), 'Co-evolution of Capitalism and Political Representation: The Choice of Electoral Systems', *American Political Science Review*, **104**, 393–403.

Daunton, M. J. (1995), *Progress and Poverty: An Economic and Social History of Britain, 1700–1850*. Oxford: Oxford University Press.

(2002), *Just Taxes: The Politics of Taxation in Britain, 1914–1979*. Cambridge: Cambridge University Press.

David, P. A. (1991), 'Computer and Dynamo: The Modern Productivity Paradox in a Not-Too-Distant Mirror', in OECD, *Technology and Productivity: the Challenge for Economic Policy, 315–347*. Paris: OECD.

(1994), 'Why Are Institutions the "Carriers of History"? Path Dependence and the Evolution of Conventions, Organizations and Institutions', *Structural Change and Economic Dynamics*, **5**, 205–220.

Davies, R., Haldane, A. G., Nielsen, M. and Pezzini, S. (2014), 'Measuring the Costs of Short-Termism', *Journal of Financial Stability*, **12**, 16–25.

Deane, P. and Cole, W. A. (1962), *British Economic Growth, 1688–1959*. Cambridge: Cambridge University Press.

De Jong, H. and Woltjer, P. (2011), 'Depression Dynamics: A New Estimate of the Anglo-American Manufacturing Productivity Gap in the Interwar Years', *Economic History Review*, **64**, 472–492.

DeLong, J. B. (1991), 'Did J. P. Morgan's Men Add Value? An Economist's Perspective on Financial Capitalism', in P. Temin (ed.), *Inside the Business Enterprise: Historical Perspectives on the Use of Information*. Chicago: University of Chicago Press, 205–250.

Dickerson, A. P., Gibson, H. D. and Tsakalotos, E. (1998), 'Takeover Risk and Dividend Strategy: A Study of UK Firms', *Journal of Industrial Economics*, **46**, 281–300.

Dutton, H. I. (1984), *The Patent System and Inventive Activity*. Manchester: Manchester University Press.

Edelstein, M. (1982), *Overseas Investment in the Age of High Imperialism: The United Kingdom, 1850–1914*. New York: Columbia University Press.

Edgerton, D. (1996), *Science, Technology and the British Industrial 'Decline'*. Cambridge: Cambridge University Press.

Edgerton, D. E. H. and Horrocks, S. (1994), 'British Industrial Research and Development Before 1945', *Economic History Review*, **47**, 213–238.

Edquist, H. (2010), 'Does Hedonic Price Indexing Change our Interpretation of Economic History? Evidence from Swedish Electrification', *Economic History Review*, **63**, 500–523.

Edwards, J. R. (1989), *A History of Financial Accounting*. London: Routledge.

Edwards, J. and Ogilvie, S. (1996), 'Universal Banks and German Industrialization: A Reappraisal', *Economic History Review*, **49**, 427–446.

Eggertsson, G. B. (2012), 'Was the New Deal Contractionary?' *American Economic Review*, **102**, 524–555.

Eichengreen, B. (1996), 'Institutions and Economic Growth: Europe After World War II', in N. Crafts and G. Toniolo (eds.), *Economic Growth in Europe Since 1945*. Cambridge: Cambridge University Press, 38–72.

(2007), *The European Economy Since 1945*. Princeton: Princeton University Press.

Eichengreen, B. and Boltho, A. (2008), 'The Economic Impact of European Integration', CEPR Discussion Paper No. 6820.

Elbaum, B. and Lazonick, W. (1986), 'An Institutional Perspective on British Decline', in B. Elbaum and W. Lazonick (eds.), *The Decline of the British Economy*. Oxford: Clarendon Press, 1–17.

Ennew, C., Greenaway, D. and Reed, G. (1990), 'Further Evidence on Effective Tariffs and Effective Protection in the UK', *Oxford Bulletin of Economics and Statistics*, **52**, 69–78.

Feinstein, C. H. (1972), *National Income, Expenditure and Output of the United Kingdom, 1855–1965*. Cambridge: Cambridge University Press.

(1981), 'Capital Accumulation and the Industrial Revolution', in R. Floud and D. N. McCloskey (eds.), *The Economic History of Britain Since 1700*, vol. **1**. Cambridge: Cambridge University Press, 128–142.

Feinstein, C. H., Matthews, R. C. O. and Odling-Smee, J. C. (1982), 'The Timing of the Climacteric and Its Sectoral Incidence in the UK, 1873–1913', in C. P. Kindleberger and G. di Tella (eds.), *Economics in the Long View: Essays in Honour of W. W. Rostow*, vol. **2**. London: Macmillan, 168–185.

Fernandez, R. and Rodrik, D. (1991), 'Resistance to Reform: Status-Quo Bias in the Presence of Individual-Specific Uncertainty', *American Economic Review*, **81**, 1146–1155.

Field, Alexander J. (2011), *A Great Leap Forward: 1930s Depression and U.S. Economic Growth*. New Haven, CT: Yale University Press.

Flanagan, R. J., Soskice, D. W. and Ulman, L. (1983), *Unionism, Economic Stabilization, and Incomes Policies: European Experience*. Washington, DC: The Brookings Institution.

Florence, P. S. (1961), *Ownership, Control and Success of Large Companies: An Analysis of English Industrial Structure and Policy 1936–1951*. London: Sweet and Maxwell.

Fohlin, C. (2012), *Mobilizing Money*. Cambridge: Cambridge University Press.

Foreman-Peck, J. (1990), 'The 1856 Companies Act and the Birth and Death of Firms', in P. Jobert and M. Moss (eds.), *The Birth and Death of Companies: An Historical Perspective*. Carnforth: Parthenon Publishing Group, 33–46.

Foreman-Peck, J. and Hannah, L. (2012), 'Extreme Divorce: The Managerial Revolution in UK Companies Before 1914', *Economic History Review*, **65**, 1217–1238.

(2013), 'Some Consequences of the Early Twentieth-Century British Divorce of Ownership from Control', *Business History*, **55**, 543–564.

Franks, J., Mayer, C. and Rossi, S. (2009), 'Ownership: Evolution and Regulation', *Review of Financial Studies*, **22**, 4009–4056.

Frontier Economics (2014), *Rates of Return to Investment in Science and Innovation*. London.

Gardner, N. (1976), 'The Economics of Launching Aid', in A. Whiting (ed.), *The Economics of Industrial Subsidies*. London: HMSO.

Garside, W. R. (1990), *British Unemployment 1919–1939*. Cambridge: Cambridge University Press.

Geroski, P. (1990), 'Innovation, Technological Opportunity, and Market Structure', *Oxford Economic Papers*, **42**, 586–602.

Geroski, P. and Jacquemin, A. (1988), 'The Persistence of Profits: A European Comparison', *Economic Journal*, **98**, 375–389.

Gerschenkron, A. (1962), *Economic Backwardness in Historical Perspective*. Cambridge, MA: Belknap Press.

Gilmore, O. (2009), 'Corporatism and Growth: Testing the Eichengreen Hypothesis', MSc Dissertation, University of Warwick.

Goetzmann, W. N. and Ukhov, A. D. (2006), 'British Investment Overseas 1870–1913: A Modern Portfolio Theory Approach', *Review of Finance*, **10**, 261–300.

Goldin, C. and Katz, L. F. (1999), 'The Shaping of Higher Education: The Formative Years in the United States, 1890–1940', *Journal of Economic Perspectives*, **13**(1), 37–62.

(2008), *The Race Between Education and Technology*. Cambridge, MA: Harvard University Press.

Goodhart, C. A. E. and Bhansali, R. J. (1970), 'Political Economy', *Political Studies*, **18**, 43–106.

Gospel, H. (2005), 'Markets, Firms and Unions', in S. Fernie and D. Metcalf (eds.), *Trade Unions: Resurgence or Demise?* Abingdon: Routledge, 19–44.

Greasley, D. and Oxley, L. (1996), 'Discontinuities in Competitiveness: The Impact of the First World War on British Industry', *Economic History Review*, **49**, 82–100.

Green, R. and Haskel, J. (2004), 'Seeking a Premier-League Economy: The Role of Privatization', in D. Card, R. Blundell, and R. Freeman (eds.), *Seeking a Premier Economy: The Effects of British Economic Reforms, 1980–2000*. Chicago: University of Chicago Press, 63–108.

Greenaway, D. and Milner, C. (1994), 'Determinants of the Inter-Industry Structure of Protection in the UK', *Oxford Bulletin of Economics and Statistics*, **56**, 399–419.

Gregg, P., Machin, S. and Metcalf, D. (1993), 'Signals and Cycles: Productivity Growth and Change in Union Status in British Companies, 1984–9', *Economic Journal*, **103**, 894–907.

Griffith, R. (2001), 'Product Market Competition, Efficiency and Agency Costs: An Empirical Analysis', Institute for Fiscal Studies Working Paper No. 01/12.

Griffith, R., Redding, S. and van Reenen, J. (2001), 'Measuring the Cost-Effectiveness of an R & D Tax Credit for the UK', *Fiscal Studies*, **22**, 375–399.

Guinnane, T. (2002), 'Delegated Monitors, Large and Small: Germany's Banking System, 1890–1914', *Journal of Economic Literature*, **40**, 73–124.

Guinnnane, T., Harris, R. and Lamoreaux, N. (2014), 'Contractual Freedom and the Evolution of Corporate Control in Britain, 1862 to 1929', NBER Working Paper No. 20481.

Gust, C. and Marquez, J. (2004), 'International Comparisons of Productivity Growth: The Role of Information Technology and Regulatory Practices', *Labour Economics*, **11**, 33–58.

Habakkuk, H. J. (1962), *American and British Technology in the Nineteenth Century*. Cambridge: Cambridge University Press.

Haldane, A. G. (2017), 'Productivity Puzzles'. Speech at London School of Economics, March 20. www.bankofengland.co.uk/publications/Pages/spee ches/2017/968.aspx

Hall, P. A. and Soskice, D. (2001), 'An Introduction to Varieties of Capitalism', in P. A. Hall and D. Soskice (eds.), *Varieties of Capitalism*. Oxford: Oxford University Press, 1–68.

Hannah, L. (1974), 'Takeover Bids in Britain Before 1950: An Exercise in Business Pre-History', *Business History*, **16**, 65–77.

  (1983), *The Rise of the Corporate Economy*. London: Methuen.

  (2014), 'Corporations in the US and Europe, 1790–1860', *Business History*, **56**, 865–899.

  (2015), 'A Global Corporate Census: Publicly Traded and Close Companies in 1910', *Economic History Review*, **68**, 548–573.

Hanushek, E. A. and Woessmann, L. (2012), 'Do Better Schools Lead to More Growth? Cognitive Skills, Economic Outcomes, and Education', *Journal of Economic Growth*, **17**, 267–321.

Harley, C. K. (2013), 'British and European Industrialization', University of Oxford Discussion Paper in Economic and Social History No. 111.

Harley, C. K. and Crafts, N. (2000), "Simulating the Two Views of the Industrial Revolution', *Journal of Economic History*, **60**, 819–841.

Harris, J. R. (1976), 'Skills, Coal and British Industry in the Eighteenth Century', *History*, **61**, 167–182.

Harris, R. (2000), *Industrializing English Law: Entrepreneurship and Business Organization, 1720-1844*. Cambridge: Cambridge University Press.

Harris, R., Siegel, D. S. and Wright, M. (2005), 'Assessing the Impact of Management Buyouts on Economic Efficiency: Plant-Level Evidence from the United Kingdom', *Review of Economics and Statistics*, **87**, 148–153.

Hart, P. E. (1968), 'A Long-Run Analysis of the Rate of Return on Capital in Manufacturing Industry, United Kingdom, 1920–62', in Hart, P. E. (ed.), *Studies in Profit, Business Saving and Investment in the United Kingdom, 1920–1962*. London: George Allen & Unwin, 220–283.

Haskel, J. (1991), 'Imperfect Competition, Work Practices and Productivity Growth', *Oxford Bulletin of Economics and Statistics*, **53**, 265–279.

Haskel, J. and Sadun, R. (2012), 'Regulation and UK Retailing Productivity: Evidence from Micro-Data', *Economica*, **79**, 425–448.

Hatton, T. J. and Thomas, M. (2013), 'Labour Markets in Recession and Recovery: The UK and the USA in the 1920s and 1930s', in N. Crafts and P. Fearon (eds.), *The Great Depression of the 1930s: Lessons for Today*. Oxford: Oxford University Press, 328–357.

Haydu, J. (1988), 'Employers, Unions, and American Exceptionalism: Pre-World War I Open Shops in the Machine Trades in Comparative Perspective', *International Journal of Social History*, **33**, 25–41.

Helm, D. and Tindall, T. (2009), 'The Evolution of Infrastructure and Utility Ownership and Its Implications', *Oxford Review of Economic Policy*, **25**, 411–434.

Henderson, P. D. (1977), 'Two British Errors: Their Probable Size and Some Possible Lessons', *Oxford Economic Papers*, **29**, 159–205.

Hendry, J. (1989), *Innovating for Failure: Government Policy and the Early British Computer Industry*. London: MIT Press.

Hickson, K. (2004), 'The Postwar Consensus Revisited', *The Political Quarterly*, **75**, 142–154.

Hitiris, T. (1978), 'Effective Protection and Economic Performance in UK Manufacturing Industry, 1963 and 1968', *Economic Journal*, **88**, 107–120.

Howson, S. (1975), *Domestic Monetary Management in Britain, 1919–1938*. Cambridge: Cambridge University Press.

Huberman, M. (1991), 'Industrial Relations and the Industrial Revolution: Evidence from M'Connel and Kennedy, 1810–1840', *Business History Review*, **65**, 345–378.

Hulten, C. (1978), 'Growth Accounting with Intermediate Inputs', *Review of Economic Studies*, **45**, 511–518.

Independent Commission on Banking (2011), *Final Report*. London: The Stationery Office.

Irving, R. J. (1976), *The North-Eastern Railway Company*. Leicester: Leicester University Press.

Irwin, D. A. (2001), 'Tariffs and Growth in Late Nineteenth-Century America', *The World Economy*, **24**, 15–30.

Iversen, T. and Soskice, D. (2009), 'Distribution and Redistribution: The Shadow of the Nineteenth Century', *World Politics*, **61**, 438–486.

Janossy, F. (1969), *The End of the Economic Miracle*. White Plains, NY: IASP.

Jerzmanowski, M. (2007), 'Total Factor Productivity Differences: Appropriate Technology vs. Efficiency', *European Economic Review*, **51**, 2080–2110.

Jones, R. (1987), *Wages and Employment Policy, 1936–1985*. London: Allen & Unwin.

Kamps, C. (2005), 'Is There a Lack of Public Capital in the European Union?' *EIB Papers*, **10**(1), 73–93.

Kanefsky, J. (1979), 'The Diffusion of Power Technology in British Industry'. Unpublished PhD Dissertation, University of Exeter.

Kavanagh, D. and Morris, P. (1994), 'The Rise and Fall of Consensus Politics', in D. Kavanagh and P. Morris (eds.), *Consensus Politics from Attlee to Major*. Oxford: Blackwell, 1–22.

Kendrick, J. W. (1961), *Productivity Trends in the United States*. Princeton, NJ: Princeton University Press.

Kennedy, W. P. (1987), *Industrial Structure, Capital Markets and the Origins of British Industrial Decline*. Cambridge: Cambridge University Press.

King, M. A. and Fullerton, D. (1984), *The Taxation of Income from Capital*. Chicago: University of Chicago Press.

King, M. A. and Robson, M. H. (1993), 'United Kingdom', in D. W. Jorgenson and R. Landau (eds.), *Tax Reform and the Cost of Capital*. Washington DC: The Brookings Institution, 300–332.

Kitson, M. and Solomou, S. (1990), *Protectionism and Economic Revival*. Cambridge: Cambridge University Press.

Kitson, M., Solomou, S. and Weale, M. (1991), 'Effective Protection and Economic Recovery in the United Kingdom During the 1930s', *Economic History Review*, **44**, 328–338.

Kuznets, S. (1966), *Modern Economic Growth: Rate, Structure, and Spread*. New Haven: Yale University Press.

Landes, D. S. (1998), *The Wealth and Poverty of Nations*. London: Little Brown.

Lazonick, W. (1994), 'Employment Relations in Manufacturing and International Competition', in R. C. Floud and D. N. McCloskey (eds.), *The Economic History of Britain Since 1700*, vol. **2**. Cambridge: Cambridge University Press, 90–116.

Lee, C. H. (1979), *British Regional Employment Statistics, 1841–1971*. Cambridge: Cambridge University Press.

Leunig, T. (2001), 'New Answers to Old Questions: Explaining the Slow Adoption of Ring Spinning in Lancashire, 1890–1913', *Journal of Economic History*, **61**, 439–466.

Lewchuk, W. (1987), *American Technology and the British Vehicle Industry*. Cambridge: Cambridge University Press.

Lipsey, R. G., Bekar, C. and Carlaw, K. (1998), 'The Consequences of Changes in GPTs', in E. Helpman (ed.), *General Purpose Technologies and Economic Growth*. Cambridge, MA: MIT Press, 193–218.

Lowe, R. (1987), 'The Government and Industrial Relations, 1919–39', in C. Wrigley (ed.), *A History of British Industrial Relations*, vol. **2**, 1914–1939. Brighton: Harvester Press, 185–210.

Lupton, T. (1963), *On the Shop Floor*. Oxford: Pergamon Press.

Macallan, C., Millard, S. and Parker, M. (2008), 'The Cyclicality of Mark-ups and Profit Margins for the United Kingdom: Some New Evidence', Bank of England Working Paper No. 351.

Machin, S. and Wadhwani, S. (1989), 'The Effects of Unions on Organisational Change, Investment and Employment: Evidence from WIRS Data', London School of Economics Centre for Labour Economics Discussion Paper No. 355.

Macmillan, H. (1938), *The Middle Way*. London: Macmillan.

Maddison, A. (1992), 'A Long-Run Perspective on Saving', *Scandinavian Journal of Economics*, **94**, 181–196.

(1996), 'Macroeconomic Accounts for European Countries', in B. van Ark and N. Crafts (eds.), *Quantitative Aspects of Postwar European Economic Growth*. Cambridge: Cambridge University Press, 27–83.

(2010), *Historical Statistics of the World Economy, 1-2008AD*. www.ggdc.net /maddison

Magee, G. (2004), 'Manufacturing and Technological Change', in R. Floud and P. Johnson (eds.), *The Cambridge Economic History of Modern Britain*, vol. **2**. Cambridge: Cambridge University Press, 74–98.

Matthews, R. C. O., Feinstein, C. H. and Odling-Smee, J. C. (1982), *British Economic Growth 1856-1973*. Stanford: Stanford University Press.

McCloskey, D. N. (1970), 'Did Victorian Britain Fail?' *Economic History Review*, **23**, 446–459.

(1981), 'The Industrial Revolution: A Survey', in R. Floud and D. N. McCloskey (eds.), *The Economic History of Britain Since 1700*, vol. 1. Cambridge: Cambridge University Press, 103–127.

McCloskey, D. N. and Sandberg, L. G. (1971), 'From Damnation to Redemption: Judgments on the Late Victorian Entrepreneur', *Explorations in Economic History*, **9**, 89–108.

McKinlay, A. and Zeitlin, J. (1989), 'The Meanings of Managerial Prerogative: Industrial Relations and the Organisation of Work in British Engineering, 1880–1939', *Business History*, **31**, 32–47.

Meeks, G. (1977), *Disappointing Marriage*. Cambridge: Cambridge University Press.

Mercer, H. (1995), *Constructing a Competitive Order: The Hidden History of British Antitrust Policies*. Cambridge: Cambridge University Press.

Metcalf, D. (2005), 'Trade Unions: Resurgence or Perdition?' in S. Fernie and D. Metcalf (eds.), *Trade Unions: Resurgence or Demise?* Abingdon: Routledge, 83–117.

Middleton, R. (1996), *Government Versus the Market*. Cheltenham: Edward Elgar.

Miles, D. (1993), 'Testing for Short-Termism in the UK Stock Market', *Economic Journal*, **103**, 1379–1396.

Miles, D., Yang, J. and Marcheggiano, G. (2013), 'Optimal Bank Capital', *Economic Journal*, **123**, 1–37.

Mills, T. C. (1991), 'Are Output Fluctuations in the UK Transitory or Permanent?' *The Manchester School*, **59**, 1–11.

Mills, T. C. and Crafts, N. (2000), 'After the Golden Age: A Long-Run Perspective on Growth Rates that Speeded Up, Slowed Down, and Still Differ', *The Manchester School*, **68**, 68–91.

Millward, R. (1997), 'The 1940s Nationalizations in Britain: Means to an End or the Means of Production?' *Economic History Review*, **50**, 209–234.

Mitch, D. (1999), 'The Role of Education and Skill in the Industrial Revolution', in J. Mokyr (ed.), *The British Industrial Revolution: An Economic Perspective*. Oxford: Westview Press, 241–279.

Mitchell, B. R. (1988), *British Historical Statistics*. Cambridge: Cambridge University Press.

Mokyr, J. (1990), *The Lever of Riches*. Oxford: Oxford University Press.
(2002), *The Gifts of Athena*. Princeton: Princeton University Press.
(2009), *The Enlightened Economy: An Economic History of Britain 1700–1850*. New Haven: Yale University Press.

Morgan, A. D. and Martin, D. (1975), 'Tariff Reductions and UK Imports of Manufactures, 1955–1971', *National Institute Economic Review*, **72**, 38–54.

Morris, D. (1998), 'The Stock Market and Problems of Corporate Control in the United Kingdom', in T. Buxton, P. Chapman and P. Temple (eds.), *Britain's Economic Performance*, 2nd edition. London: Routledge, 200–252.

Morris, D. J. and Stout, D. (1985), 'Industrial Policy', in D. J. Morris (ed.), *The Economic System in the UK*. Oxford: Oxford University Press, 851–894.

Morrisson, C. and Murtin, F. (2009), 'The Century of Education', *Journal of Human Capital*, **3**, 1–42.

Mosley, P. (1984), *The Making of Economic Policy: Theory and Evidence from Britain and the United States Since 1945*. Brighton: Wheatsheaf Books.

Mowery, D. C. and Rosenberg, N. (2000), 'Twentieth Century Technological Change', in S. L. Engerman and R. E. Gallmann (eds.), *The Cambridge Economic History of the United States*, vol. **3**. Cambridge: Cambridge University Press, 803–925.

Murray, J. (2014), 'Output Gap Measurement: Judgement and Uncertainty', Office for Budget Responsibility Working Paper No. 5.

NEDO (1976), *A Study of UK Nationalised Industries*. London: HMSO (Her Majesty's Stationery Office).

Nelson, R. R. and Wright, G. (1992), 'The Rise and Fall of American Technological Leadership: The Postwar Era in Historical Perspective', *Journal of Economic Literature* **30**, 1931–1964.

Newbould, G. D. (1970), *Management and Merger Activity*. Liverpool: Guthstead.

Nicholas, T. (2010), 'The Role of Independent Invention in U.S. Technological Development, 1880–1930', *Journal of Economic History*, **70**, 57–82.

(2011), 'Independent Invention During the Rise of the Corporate Economy in Britain and Japan', *Economic History Review*, **64**, 995–1023.

Nickell, S. J. (1996), 'Competition and Corporate Performance', *Journal of Political Economy*, **104**, 724–746.

Nickell, S. J., Nicolitsas, D. and Dryden, N. (1997), 'What Makes Firms Perform Well?' *European Economic Review*, **41**, 783–796.

Nicoletti, G. and Scarpetta, S. (2003), 'Regulation, Productivity and Growth', *Economic Policy*, **36**, 9–72.

Niemi, A. W. (1974), *State and Regional Patterns in American Manufacturing, 1860–1900*. Westport, CT: Greenwood Press.

Nordhaus, W. D. (1972), 'The Recent Productivity Slowdown', *Brookings Papers on Economic Activity*, **3**, 493–531.

North, D. C. (2005), *Understanding the Process of Economic Change*. Princeton, NJ: Princeton University Press.

Nyman, S. and Silberston, A. (1978), 'The Ownership and Control of Industry', *Oxford Economic Papers*, **30**, 74–101.

O'Brien, P. K. (1996), 'Path Dependency, or Why Britain Became an Industrialized and Urbanized Economy Long Before France', *Economic History Review*, **49**, 213–249.

OECD (1991), *Main Science and Technology Indicators*. Paris: OECD.

O'Mahony, M. (1999), *Britain's Productivity Performance, 1950–1996*. London: NIESR.

O'Rourke, K. H. (1997), 'The European Grain Invasion', *Journal of Economic History*, **57**, 775–801.

O'Rourke, K. H. and Williamson, J. G. (2002), 'When Did Globalization Begin?' *European Review of Economic History*, **6**, 23–50.

Oulton, N. (2012), 'Long-Term Implications of the ICT Revolution: Applying the Lessons of Growth Theory and Growth Accounting', *Economic Modelling*, **29**, 1722–1736.

(2013), 'Has the Growth of Real GDP in the UK been Overstated Because of Mismeasurement of Banking Output?' *National Institute Economic Review*, **224**, R59–R65.

Oulton, N. and Sebastia-Barriel, M. (2017), 'Effects of Financial Crises on Productivity, Capital and Employment', *Review of Income and Wealth*, **63**, S90–S112.

Owens, J. and Whitehouse, E. (1996), 'Tax Reform for the 21st Century', *Bulletin of International Fiscal Documentation*, **50**, 538–547.

Patterson, C., Sahin, A., Topa, G. and Violante, G. L. (2016), 'Working Hard in the Wrong Place: A Mismatch-Based Explanation to the UK Productivity Puzzle', *European Economic Review*, **84**, 42–56.

Phelps Brown, E. H. (1983), *The Origins of Trade Union Power*. Oxford: Clarendon Press.

Pilgrim Trust (1938), *Men Without Work*. Cambridge: Cambridge University Press.

Pollard, S. (1989), *Britain's Prime and Britain's Decline: The British Economy, 1870–1914*. London: Edward Arnold.

(1992), *The Development of the British Economy, 1914–1990*. London: Edward Arnold.

Prais, S. J. (1981), *Productivity and Industrial Structure*. Cambridge, Cambridge University Press.

Pratten, C. F. (1976), *Labour Productivity Differentials Within International Companies*. Cambridge: Cambridge University Press.

Pratten, C. F. and Atkinson, A. G. (1976), 'The Use of Manpower in British Industry', *Department of Employment Gazette*, **84**, 571–576.

Price, S. and Sanders, D. (1993), 'Modeling Government Popularity in Postwar Britain: A Methodological Example', *American Journal of Political Science*, **37**, 317–334.

Proudman, J. and Redding, S. (1998), 'A Summary of the Openness and Growth Project', in J. Proudman and S. Redding (eds.), *Openness and Growth*. London: Bank of England, 1–29.

Radice, H. (1971), 'Control Type, Profitability and Growth in Large Firms: An Empirical Study', *Economic Journal*, **81**, 547–562.

Reinhart, C. M. and Rogoff, K. S. (2014), 'Recovery from Financial Crises: Evidence from 100 Episodes', *American Economic Review Papers and Proceedings*, **104**(5), 50–55.

Richardson, H. W. (1965), 'Over-Commitment in Britain Before 1930', *Oxford Economic Papers*, **17**, 237–262.

(1967), *Economic Recovery in Britain, 1932–1939*. London: Weidenfeld and Nicolson.

Ristuccia, C. A. and Solomou, S. (2014), 'Can General Purpose Technology Theory Explain Economic Growth? Electrical Power as a Case Study', *European Review of Economic History*, **18**, 227–247.

Rollings, N. (2007), *British Business in the Formative Years of European Integration, 1945–1973*. Cambridge: Cambridge University Press.

Root, H. (1991), 'The Redistributive Role of Government Economic Regulation in Old Regime France and England', *Comparative Studies in Society and History*, **33**, 338–369.

Rubinstein, W. D. (1987), *Elites and the Wealthy in Modern British History*, Brighton: Harvester Press.

(1992), 'The Structure of Wealth-Holding in Britain, 1809–39: A Preliminary Anatomy', *Historical Research*, 65, 74–89.

Sanders, D. (1996), 'Economic Performance, Management Competence and the Outcome of the Next General Election', *Political Studies*, **44**, 203–231.

Sanderson, M. (1988), 'Education and Economic Decline, 1890-1980s', *Oxford Review of Economic Policy*, **4**(1), 38–50.

Schularick, M. and Solomou, S. (2011), 'Tariffs and Economic Growth in the First Era of Globalization', *Journal of Economic Growth*, **16**, 33–70.

Scott, P. (2002), 'Towards the "Cult of the Equity"? Insurance Companies and the Interwar Capital Market', *Economic History Review*, **55**, 78–104.

Scott, P. and Walsh, P. (2005), 'New Manufacturing Plant Formation, Clustering and Locational Externalities in 1930s Britain', *Business History*, **47**, 190–218.

Sefton, J. and Weale, M. (1995), *Reconciliation of National Income and Expenditure*. Cambridge: Cambridge University Press.

Shaw-Taylor, L. (2009), 'The Occupational Structure of England and Wales, 1750–1871: A Preliminary Report', Cambridge Group for the History of Population and Social Structure Occupations Project Paper No. 19.

Shleifer, A. (1998), 'State Versus Private Ownership', *Journal of Economic Perspectives*, **12**(4), 133–150.

Short, H. and Keasey, K. (2005), 'Institutional Shareholders and Corporate Governance in the UK', in K. Keasey, S. Thompson and M. Wright (eds.), *Corporate Governance: Accountability, Enterprise and International Comparisons*. Chichester: John Wiley and Sons, 61–95.

Singh, A. (1975), 'Takeovers, Natural Selection and the Theory of the Firm', *Economic Journal*, **85**, 497–515.

Solomou, S. and Weale, M. (1991), 'Balanced Estimates of UK GDP, 1870–1913', *Explorations in Economic History*, **28**, 54–63.

Sullivan, R. J. (1994), 'Estimates of the Value of Patent Rights in Britain and Ireland, 1852–1876', *Economica*, **61**, 37–58.

Sumner, M. (1999), 'Long-Run Effects of Investment Incentives', in C. Driver and P. Temple (eds.), *Investment, Growth and Employment: Perspectives for Policy*. London: Routledge, 292–300.

Supple, B. E. (1987), *History of the British Coal Industry*, vol. **4**, 1913–1946. Oxford: Oxford University Press.

Symeonidis, G. (2008), 'The Effects of Competition on Wages and Productivity: Evidence from the United Kingdom', *Review of Economics and Statistics*, **90**, 134–146.

Tanzi, V. (1969), *The Individual Income Tax and Economic Growth*. Baltimore, MD: Johns Hopkins University Press.

Temin, P. (2002), 'The Golden Age of European Growth Reconsidered', *European Review of Economic History*, **6**, 3–22.

Temin, P. and Voth, H. J. (2013), *Prometheus Shackled*. Oxford: Oxford University Press.

Tena-Junguito, A. (2010), 'Bairoch Revisited: Tariff Structure and Growth in the Late Nineteenth Century', *European Review of Economic History*, **14**, 111–143.

The Conference Board (2016), *Total Economy Database*. www.conference-board .org/data/economy/database/

Thomas, M. (1983), 'Rearmament and Economic Recovery in the Late 1930s', *Economic History Review*, **36**, 552–579.

(1984), 'An Input-Output Approach to the British Economy, 1890–1914', D Phil. Thesis, University of Oxford.

(1988), 'Slowdown in the Pre-World War One Economy', *Oxford Review of Economic Policy*, **4**(1), 14–24.

Tolliday, S. (1987), *Business, Banking and Politics: The Case of British Steel*. Cambridge: Cambridge University Press.

Tomlinson, J. (1996), 'Inventing "Decline": The Falling Behind of the British Economy in the Postwar Years', *Economic History Review*, **49**, 731–757.

Toms, S., Wilson, N. and Wright, M. (2015), 'The Evolution of Private Equity: Corporate Restructuring in the UK, c. 1945–2010', *Business History*, **57**, 736–768.

van Ark, B. (2011), 'Up the Hill and Down Again: A History of Europe's Productivity Gap Relative to the United States, 1950–2009', *Nordic Economic Policy Review*, **2**, 27–56.

van Ark, B., Hao, J. X., Corrado, C. and Hulten, C. (2009), 'Measuring Intangible Capital and Its Contribution to Economic Growth in Europe', *EIB Papers*, **14**(1), 63–93.

Van Reenen, J. (2013), 'Productivity Under the 1997–2010 Labour Government', *Oxford Review of Economic Policy*, **29**, 113–141.

Verspagen, B. (1996), 'Technology Indicators and Economic Growth in the European Area: Some Empirical Evidence', in B. van Ark and N. Crafts (eds.), *Quantitative Aspects of Postwar European Economic Growth*. Cambridge: Cambridge University Press, 215–243.

Vickers, J. and Yarrow, G. (1988), *Privatization: An Economic Analysis*. Cambridge, MA: MIT Press.

Von Tunzelmann, G. N. (1978), *Steam Power and British Industrialization to 1860*. Oxford: Clarendon Press.

Voth, H.-J. (2001), 'The Longest Years: New Estimates of Labor Input in England, 1760–1830', *Journal of Economic History*, **61**, 1065–1082.

Wallis, J. and Dollery, B. (1999), *Market Failure, Government Failure, Leadership and Public Policy*. London: Macmillan.

Wallis, P. (2014), 'Labour Markets and Training', in R. Floud, J. Humphries and P. Johnson (eds.), *The Cambridge Economic History of Modern Britain, Vol. 1: 1700–1870*. Cambridge: Cambridge University Press, 178–210.

Warwick, K. (2013), 'Beyond Industrial Policy', OECD STI Policy Paper No. 2.

Woessmann, L. (2016), 'The Importance of School Systems: Evidence from International Differences in Student Achievement', *Journal of Economic Perspectives*, **30**(3), 3–32.

Woltjer, P. J. (2013), 'Taking Over: a New US/UK Productivity Benchmark and the Nature of American Leadership c. 1910', Groningen Growth and Development Centre Research Memorandum No. 140.

Wren, C. (1996a), 'Grant-Equivalent Expenditure on Industrial Subsidies in the Postwar United Kingdom', *Oxford Bulletin of Economics and Statistics*, **58**, 317–353.

Wren, C. (1996b), *Industrial Subsidies: the UK Experience*. London: Macmillan.

Wren, C. (2001), 'The Industrial Policy of Competitiveness: A Review of Recent Developments in the UK', *Regional Studies*, **35**, 847–860.

Wrigley, C. (2002), *British Trade Unions Since 1933*. Cambridge: Cambridge University Press.

Zweig, F. (1951), *Productivity and Trade Unions*. Oxford: Basil Blackwell.

Index

agglomeration, 33, 53
agriculture, 11, 13, 15, 29, 55, 80, 102

banking, 25, 34, 49, 120, 121, 122

capital, 4, 5, 6, 7, 16, 18, 20, 24, 33, 34, 49, 50,
    56, 57, 59, 64, 73, 84, 86, 101, 103,
    106, 111, 115, 118, 119, 120, 125
capital deepening, 16, 18, 26, 43, 82, 106, 121
capital market, 25, 26, 33, 34, 36, 37, 44, 46,
    47, 48
cartelization, 73, 74, 93
catch-up growth, 4, 5, 8, 38, 79, 86, 98, 102,
    125, 128
climacteric, 41, 42
CME (co-ordinated market economy), 86, 87,
    88, 102, 117, 125, 128
collective bargaining, 24, 35, 57, 67, 76, 95,
    113, 127, 128
comparative advantage, 29, 33, 37, 51, 52, 58, 70
competition, 5, 9, 47, 48, 55, 60, 67, 72, 73, 74,
    76, 77, 78, 79, 86, 88, 91, 93, 94, 96,
    97, 98, 99, 108, 109, 112, 113, 114,
    117, 118, 121, 126, 127, 128
competition policy, 74
co-operative equilibrium, 100, 101
corporate governance, 34, 55, 59, 75, 76, 78,
    94, 97, 99, 114, 115, 127
craft control, 24, 57
craft unionism, 24, 35, 57, 58, 59, 76, 127

early start, ix, 9, 12, 28, 36, 38, 52, 53, 58, 59,
    61, 68, 77, 78, 80, 88, 99, 121, 123,
    127, 128
education, 4, 12, 17, 23, 25, 40, 42, 44, 63, 64,
    83, 90, 106, 111, 115, 117, 118, 121
effort bargain, 24
electricity, 25, 40, 41, 50, 64, 90
endogenous growth, i, vi, 49
endogenous innovation, 5, 44, 45, 50, 87
entrepreneurial failure, 47
entrepreneurship, 23
exports, 14, 15, 28, 29, 33, 36, 67

finance, 34, 49, 55, 64, 86, 115, 116, 119,
    121, 127
Fordist production, 6
foreign investment, 47
free trade, 22, 28, 29, 52, 54, 60, 73, 126

general purpose technology, 20, 64, 102, 115
globalization, 23, 33, 59, 60, 79
gold standard, 60, 71
government failure, 51, 88, 90, 94, 99, 126
Great Depression, 141, 60, 62, 65, 119
growth accounting, 4, 16, 17, 39, 62, 82, 106,
    119, 123
growth potential, 12, 25, 37, 43, 45, 62, 64

Habakkuk hypothesis, 28
hold-up problems, 128
human capital, 3, 8, 17, 24, 26, 36, 45, 55, 64,
    86, 106, 115, 119, 121

ICT (information & communications
    technologies), 6, 25, 102, 103, 115,
    116, 117, 121, 125
industrial policy, 52, 60, 78, 88, 90, 99, 108,
    110, 121
industrial relations, 9, 24, 34, 35, 36, 37, 55,
    56, 57, 59, 75, 76, 78, 86, 86, 87, 94,
    96, 97, 98, 99, 108, 113, 115, 117, 118,
    121, 125, 127, 128
innovation, 7, 20, 22, 23, 25, 27, 45, 47, 51, 58,
    86, 87, 90, 97, 111, 118, 121, 125
innovative effort, 5, 6, 7, 25, 49, 50, 97
institutions, 4, 5, 6, 7, 8, 9, 12, 22, 23, 25, 27,
    28, 36, 38, 56, 58, 75, 85, 86, 94, 95,
    98, 113, 125, 127, 128
intellectual property rights, 23

labour productivity, 11, 15, 16, 18, 20, 24, 35,
    39, 43, 44, 53, 62, 70, 71, 73, 77, 79,
    82, 84, 87, 90, 93, 106, 107, 112, 115,
    117, 118, 119, 120, 124
LME (liberal market economy), 86, 87, 88, 94,
    97, 102, 117, 121, 125, 126, 127